HIDDEN HISTORY
of
CARY

HIDDEN HISTORY *of* CARY

Katherine Loflin

Published by The History Press
An imprint of Arcadia Publishing
Charleston, SC
www.historypress.com

First published 2025

Manufactured in the United States

ISBN 9781467157353

Library of Congress Control Number: 2025940390

Contents

Preface

In Cary, North Carolina, everyday life unfolds amid the familiar sounds of recycling bins being rolled up driveways, leaf blowers at work and children playing—all set against the backdrop of towering oaks and manicured yards. Yet, nestled in a quiet cul-de-sac, easily unnoticed, stands a tall obelisk grave marker. This monument, surrounded by the original and restored graves of a prominent family, speaks to the area's deep-rooted history, predating Cary's incorporation. The family arrived here before the Revolutionary War, and their patriarch was a complex man who fought valiantly in the war but lost a local election due to minimizing the resources of a rival; he was also a plantation owner whose dying wish in his will was freedom for his enslaved people. This is part of Cary's hidden history. I marvel at the juxtaposition of this centuries-old graveyard, standing in stark contrast to the modern life that surrounds it.

As I drive back to my home in Cary, just eleven minutes away, I feel the urge to share this history with every passing car, cyclist and dog walker. "Look around you!" I want to tell them. "There's history here, hidden in plain sight." Continuing up Cary Parkway, I turn onto Kildaire Farm Road and am reminded of the area's deep history—at this intersection stands the forgotten remnant of Kildaire Farm. The farm itself is long gone, but across from Trader Joe's, the cow cooling pond remains, a silent testament to the farm that once stood there.

As I continue my drive, I pass by the Wimbledon neighborhood, with its street names and logos reflecting the spirit of the famed tennis tournament.

I cross Tryon Road, named after the royal governor of North Carolina, William Tryon. This road marks the route of the one thousand troops he ordered to march from the original capital of New Bern to quell the Regulators in Orange County. They passed through what would become Cary on this very road—a journey that, many argue, set the stage for the Revolutionary War.

Farther along, I pass Lochmere, one of Cary's early planned communities, much like its predecessor, MacGregor Downs, which once served as the home for notable figures like Jim Valvano, Jim Goodnight and Lou Holtz and where Arnold Palmer played golf.

At the next intersection, I turn right, but if I turned left, I would soon be at a still standing, but hidden from view, living history farm, the Barnabas Jones Farm, dating back to before the Civil War. This land, now a Town of Cary park, also serves as a site where Native American artifacts have been found.

Instead, today I turn right and head home. My own house, too, holds history—artifact researchers believe that based on the items uncovered on my property over the years, it may have served both as a war encampment and a homestead.

Everywhere I look, I see the layered history—sometimes hidden in plain sight, sometimes tucked away and sometimes lost to time but always deserving to be told. As you turn these pages, I cannot wait for you to also learn the rich, often overlooked history that is steeped in Cary. Welcome to the hidden history of Cary.

Acknowledgements

Working in history means bearing the responsibility of preserving and sharing the stories of those who came before. I feel that responsibility deeply and take it seriously. I have immersed myself in their stories, visited their graves and asked for their guidance. My hope is that they would see this work as worthy to "Cary the stories" forward with authenticity and depth, capturing their vibrancy and complexity, so we can connect with them, see ourselves in them and keep them alive in the fabric of Cary.

History is always revealing itself, and it takes all of us to capture those revelations. The history of Cary, and this book project in particular, is no exception. I was never alone on this journey, and I'm deeply grateful for the many people who walked it with me. Conversations driven by curiosity about Cary, productions that create a new love of Cary shining in audiences' eyes, historical discoveries met with joy and shared embraces—these moments have been the most memorable part of this work.

My profound thanks to the legacy families—the direct descendants of Cary's history—who welcomed me into your homes and lives to help me understand Cary more fully. Chief among them is my Cary history mentor and dear friend Carla Jordan Michaels, a descendant of one of Cary's founding families. Carla, Cary's history would be far more hidden without your tireless dedication. I'm honored that you took me under your wing, taught me, shared your time and wisdom, encouraged me to keep going and regularly opened both your home and your research to me. You will always be my Cary history hero.

Many other legacy families also offered support, artifacts and insight, and I'm grateful to each of you: the Ashworths, Jordans, Matthewses, Iveys, Westbrooks, Ladds, Alexanders, Templetons, Roods, Evanses, Baileys, Joneses, Turners, Arringtons, Murdocks and Engrams. Your support and faith in my work truly means so much to me.

I also thank the Town of Cary for supporting my efforts. Mayor Harold Weinbrecht, thank you for being such a good sport in our productions—often stepping in as Frank Page himself—and for always asking, "What's our next production?" Your friendship and enthusiasm have added such value. Thanks as well to the Cary Town Council and Town staff—Virginia Johnson, Katie Drye, Kris Carmichael, Russ Hughes, Stefanie Nichols and Bryan Hayes—and Kerry Harville and Town Manager Sean Stegall for supporting my role as Cary's history ambassador. Gratitude also goes to other Cary-loving leaders and friends Sarah Chung, Barbara Wetmore, Anne Kratzer, Heather Leah and Dennis Midkiff.

A special note of gratitude to Ralph Ashworth, a Cary icon, for your support, trust and friendship. And to Leslie Douglas, for believing in my work from the start and being my first investor. Special thanks also to Mike Whiteside, who first introduced me to the adventure of breathing new life into history and showed me the joy of wandering to discover it.

To The City Doctor Productions family: many of you have been part of this journey from the beginning. Special gratitude to Nicholas Wendling for adventuring with me through mosquito-infested woods and oddly smelling locations, for proudly championing me to anyone who would listen, for offering your shoulder when history turned heartbreaking and for your steady presence and protection during this time. To Christina Zellis, for your fierce friendship and loyalty. To Patti Foster Clapper, for consistently going above and beyond for me. To Gail Gould, for your wisdom and support. And to J. Allen Crumpler, Crystal Stremming, Chell and Franklin Landry, Rhonda Beese, Mike Rumble, Baxter Walker, Richard Wood, Dottie Chung, Lilly Arya and the Rakolta family, thank you for consistently showing up for me and for our productions that bring Cary history to life. Thanks to my Cary history students and our production audiences for your enthusiastic support as well.

Finally, much love and heartfelt thanks to my mom, Esther Loflin, for a lifetime of unwavering love and constant "whatever you need" support, and to my beloved daughter, Bella Grace Loflin-Van Dorn—you've inspired the best version of me and fill me with pride and wonder.

Introduction

Nestled in the heart of North Carolina, Cary blends small-town charm with vibrant progress. Known for its manicured landscapes, planned communities, modern infrastructure, thriving businesses and world-class parks, Cary has long been celebrated as top place to live, a model of municipal excellence. But alongside its growth, Cary is the home of a historic downtown, the oldest surviving structures in the area and residents with direct ties to the town's founders. Today, Cary is the second-largest town in the country, but behind its rise to national prominence lies a rich history that dates back long before IBM arrived in nearby Research Triangle Park in the 1965s. Cary's past is a tapestry woven with significant history, lesser-known events and sometimes dormant narratives.

Cary's history stretches back to the Tuscarora people, whose influence still lingers today, and spans pivotal moments in the Revolutionary War, General Sherman's Civil War occupation and the significant military and diplomatic contributions of two of Cary's favorite sons during both world wars. Even before its official founding in 1871, the area served for at least a century prior as the "place in between" Raleigh and points west—or simply referred to in newspapers as "8 miles west of Raleigh." While it is said Cary stands for the humorous acronym "Containment Area for Relocated Yankees," prior to that it was jokingly said to stand for "Can't Afford Raleigh Yet." Nicknames have always been part of Cary's identity.

Initially founded as a dry town and named after a prohibitionist Yankee (instead of its actual founder), Cary held on to its prohibition status until

1964, when a threatened lawsuit from the state forced the town to approve alcohol permits. Despite its dry status, local bootleggers and moonshiners helped lay the foundation for NASCAR in North Carolina.

Few people know that Cary was a runner-up to become both North Carolina's capital and the first home of the University of North Carolina. The town is also home to the state's first public school and is the home of pioneering African Americans families whose innovative land use strategy in the Reconstruction era and beyond served as a lasting model for breaking the cycle of poverty still present in national strategies today.

Drawing on primary sources, historical records, newspaper accounts, the latest research and oral histories, this work will uncover some of the lesser-known stories that have shaped this North Carolina town.

But why is Cary's hidden history important? Beyond satisfying curiosity, understanding the layers of the town's past gives us a richer, more complete perspective on the present. It connects new arrivals, longtime residents and visitors to Cary's past, creating a bond that inspires a desire to be invested in its future. It challenges assumptions and fosters a deeper connection between the town's history and its rapid growth today.

Each chapter of this book shares history from Cary's storied past. This is not intended to be a comprehensive history, but rather a collection of lesser-known history that may inspire sharing with neighbors over the backyard fence and with strangers on airplanes. These stories will provide dimension and context to Cary's landmarks and everyday sights, turning them into historical treasures. In doing so, they become part of the town's collective history and inspire a renewed appreciation for Cary, guiding it into the future with the wisdom of its past.

Early Beginnings

The region now known as Cary, North Carolina, carries a rich tapestry of history stretching back millions of years. During the Mesozoic Era, dinosaurs and their reptilian cousins likely roamed the area, dominating the land and skies. Although fossil evidence remains elusive due to the region's dense vegetation and development, geologists confirm that fossil-producing sediments are buried across the state, including around Cary. Beneath the surface, the geological record reveals a significant fault line running under parts of nearby Raleigh, including North Carolina State University and the Angus Barn property.

Long before the rise of towns and cities, Cary's land was home to Indigenous peoples for thousands of years. Archaeological findings suggest that Native Americans inhabited the area as far back as twelve thousand years ago, with the Tuscaroras establishing a notable presence in the 1600s. The region—abundant with fertile soil, wildlife and water sources—supported thriving communities.

Artifacts unearthed across Cary provide glimpses into the lives of these early inhabitants. For instance, Jack Smith Park on Penny Road was once part of the Barnabas Jones/Bartley Farm, where descendants recall family stories that a nearby ridge housed a Tuscarora community. Plowing the fields often revealed arrowheads and other tools, some dating back three thousand to eight thousand years. Similarly, in the area now occupied by the Silverton subdivision near Cary Parkway and Evans Road, local children once collected artifacts along a creek bed, remnants of yet another Tuscarora settlement.

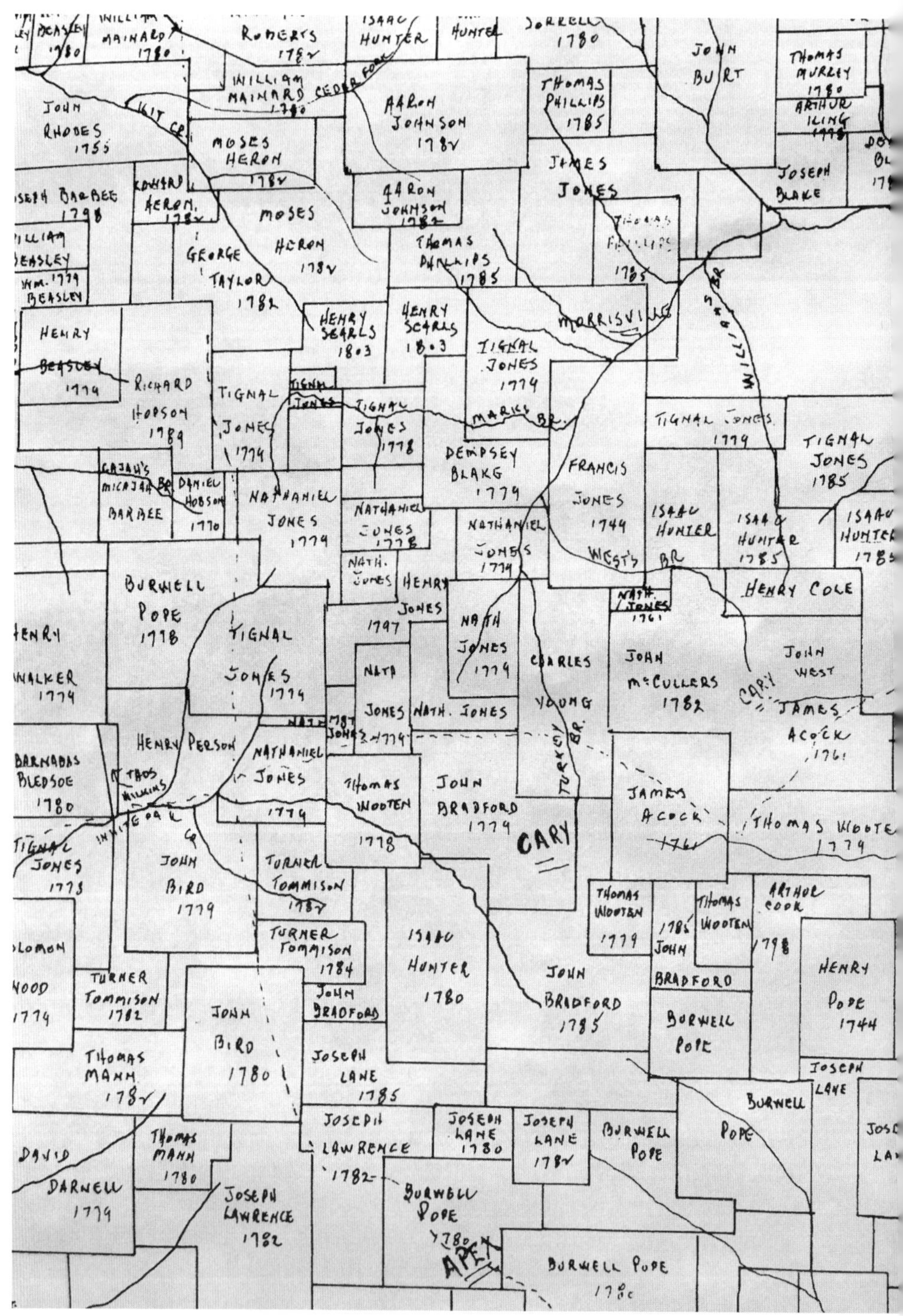
Beasley
1780
William
Mainard
1780
Roberts
1782
Isaac
Hunter
Hunter
Sorrell
1780
John
Burt
Thomas
Murrey
1780
Arthur
Iling
William
Mainard
1780
Ceder Fork
Aaron
Johnson
1782
Thomas
Phillips
1785
John
Rhodes
1755
Kit Cr.
Moses
Heron
1782
James
Jones
Joseph
Blake
Joseph Barbee
1798
Edward
Heron
1782
Moses
Heron
1782
Aaron
Johnson
1782
Thomas
Phillips
1785
William
Beasley
Wm. 1779
Beasley
George
Taylor
1782
Thomas
Phillips
1785
Henry
Searls
1803
Henry
Searls
1803
Morrisville
Williams Br.
Henry
Beasley
1779
Richard
Hobson
1789
Tignal
Jones
1779
Tignal
Jones
1779
Tignal
Jones
1778
Marks Br.
Tignal Jones
1779
Tignal
Jones
1785
Micajah's Br.
Micajah
Barbee
Daniel
Hobson
1770
Nathaniel
Jones
1779
Nathaniel
Jones
1778
Dempsey
Blake
1779
Francis
Jones
1744
Isaac
Hunter
Isaac
Hunter
1785
Isaac
Hunter
1785
Nathaniel
Jones
1779
West's Br.
Nath.
Jones
Henry
Jones
1797
Burwell
Pope
1778
Henry Cole
Nath.
Jones
1761
Henry
Walker
1779
Tignal
Jones
1779
Nath
Jones
1779
Charles
Young
John
McCullers
1782
John
West
Cary
James
Acock
1761
Nath
Jones
Nath. Jones
Henry Person
Nathaniel
Jones
1779
Turkey Br.
Barnabas
Bledsoe
1780
Thos
Wilkins
White Oak Cr.
Thomas
Wooten
1778
John
Bradford
1779
James
Acock
1761
Thomas Wooten
1779
Tignal
Jones
1773
Cary
John
Bird
1779
Turner
Tommison
1782
Thomas
Wooten
1779
Thomas
Wooten
1785
John
Bradford
Arthur
Cook
1798
Turner
Tommison
1784
Isaac
Hunter
1780
Henry
Pope
1744
Solomon
Wood
1779
Turner
Tommison
1782
John
Bradford
John
Bird
1780
John
Bradford
1785
Burwell
Pope
Thomas
Mann
1782
Joseph
Lane
1785
Joseph
Lane
Burwell
Pope
Joseph
Lawrence
1782
Joseph
Lane
1780
Joseph
Lane
1782
Burwell
Pope
David
Darnell
1779
Thomas
Mann
1780
Joseph
Lawrence
1782
Burwell
Pope
1780
Apex
Burwell Pope
1780

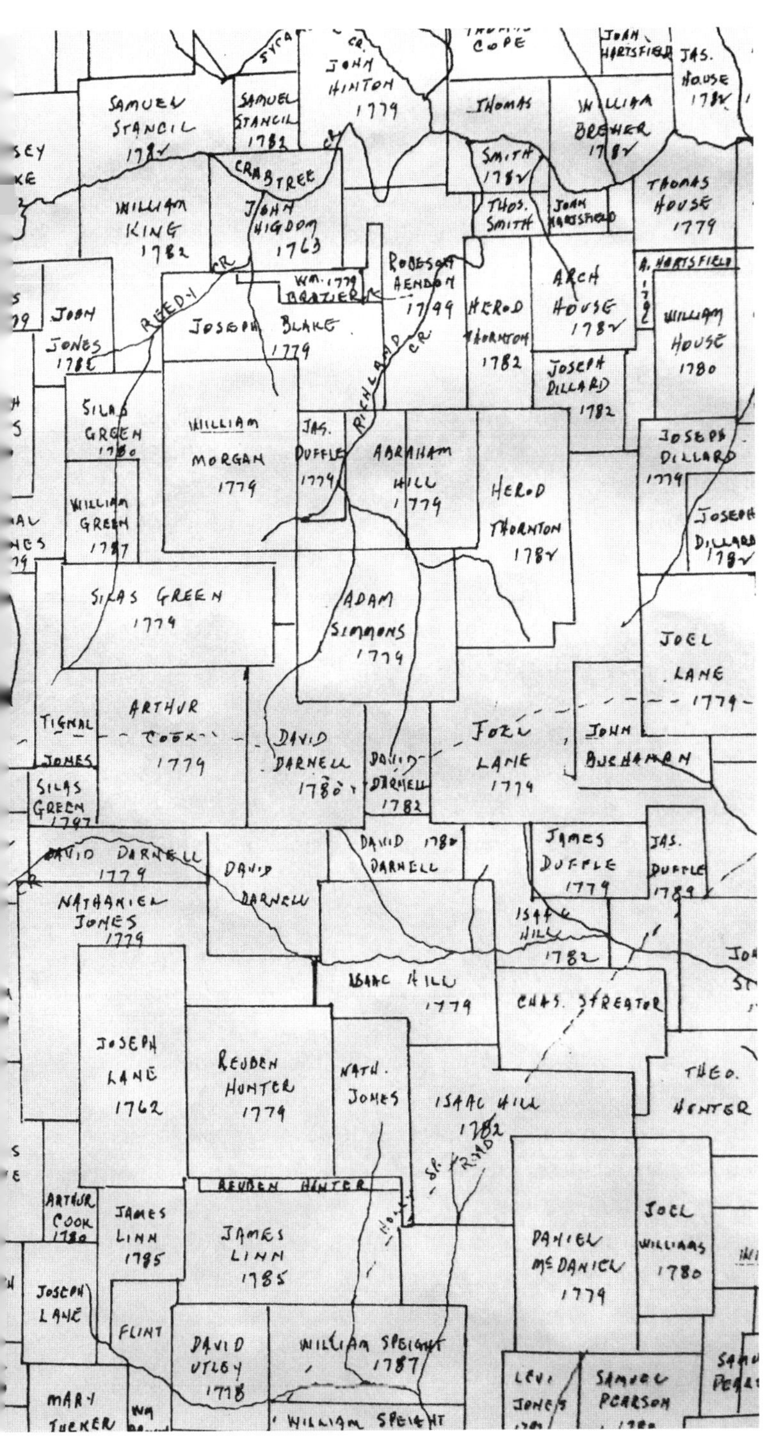

Land grant map from the 1700s of future Cary. *Allan B. Markham Estate.*

Although most of these relics are now buried under modern developments, their discovery underscores the depth of the area's history.

The Tuscarora influence extends beyond these physical artifacts. Green Level, part of Cary, derives its name from local Native Americans, who identified it as an ideal neutral meeting ground for intertribal negotiations. Its flat and verdant terrain ensured that no tribe held a tactical advantage, fostering peaceful dialogue.

However, the arrival of European settlers in the mid-1700s brought significant upheaval. Armed with land grants from British authorities, settlers claimed large swathes of land—often two hundred to three hundred acres at a time. Diseases like smallpox further decimated Indigenous populations, leading many Tuscaroras to migrate or perish. Some remained in the area, later becoming integral to Cary.

The first known European settler in what is now Cary was Francis Jones, who acquired a 640-acre land grant along Crabtree Creek in 1749. Most settlers during this period were of English descent, arriving via the Albemarle region of North Carolina. They relied on the region's vast hardwood forests, which featured tulip poplar, beech, sycamore, sweetgum, river birch and willow oaks. The original forest was eventually harvested, with the pines now prevalent in the area planted later. The land also provided sustenance through an abundance of wildlife, including wild turkeys, white-tailed deer, squirrels, elk, bison, beaver and even water buffalo.

By 1750, the area saw its first formal business establishment: Bradford's Ordinary. Owned by John Bradford, this tavern and inn occupied the site of what is now Cary's town hall. Positioned at a crossroads between New Bern and Hillsborough, as well as Raleigh and Chatham County, Bradford's Ordinary played a key role in the region's development, although much about its operations remains a mystery.

At this time, Cary's land was part of Craven County, which stretched from the coast to areas well beyond present-day Wake County. In 1746, Johnston County was carved out of Craven, encompassing the Cary area. Then, in 1771, Wake County was formed from a portion of Johnston County, establishing Cary's permanent location.

These layers of history—from prehistoric ecosystems to the settlements of Indigenous peoples and the arrival of European colonists—paint a vivid portrait of Cary's evolution. Although much has changed, the traces of the past remain embedded in the land, offering invaluable insights into the region's diverse heritage.

THE LEGACY OF THE TWO NATHANIEL JONESES

Francis Jones, a wealthy landowner originally from Virginia, made his home in Edgecombe County, North Carolina, where he established a notable family. Among his sons were Francis Jones Jr., Nathaniel Jones of Crabtree and Tignall Jones. Tignall became the father of Fanning Jones, the owner of the legendary High House, which lent its name to the road that still bears its memory. Through land grants secured between 1779 and 1801, Tignall Jones amassed significant holdings, totaling 3,779 acres across fourteen different grants. Despite his extensive acquisitions, it remains unclear if Francis Jones ever resided on this land himself. Upon his death, he bequeathed his properties to Nathaniel and Tignall, setting the stage for a legacy intertwined with Wake County's development.

Nathaniel Jones of Crabtree, the son of Nathaniel Jones Sr., inherited land along Crabtree Creek in what is now Wake County. Historical records indicate that Nathaniel Jr. received more than four thousand acres through grants between 1761 and 1800 and expanded his holdings through additional purchases. His residence, constructed between 1810 and 1820, was relocated from its original site but survives today as a private home near the Beltline and Wake Forest Road. The legacy of the Jones family is physically embodied in this structure, a testament to their influence on the area's early development.

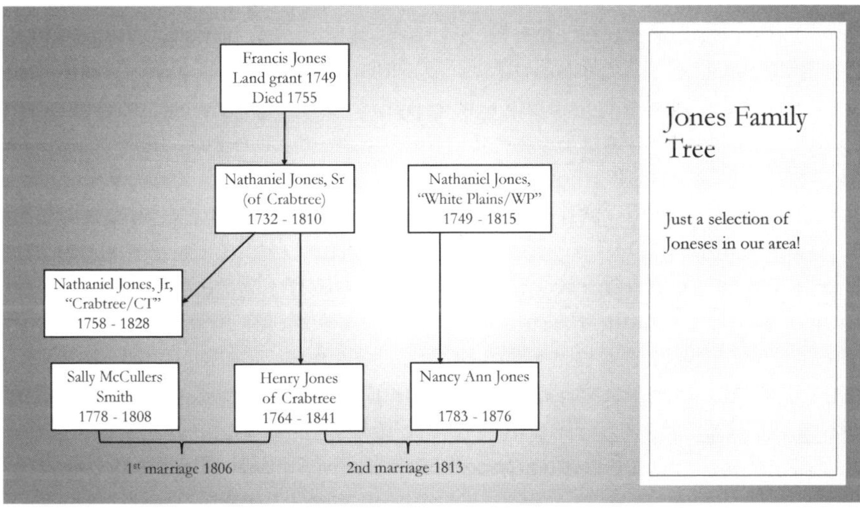

Immediate family of the two Nathaniel Joneses. *Carla Jordan Michaels.*

Nathaniel Jones of Crabtree home. *North Carolina State Historic Preservation Office.*

On the opposite side of Crabtree Creek, Nathaniel Sr.'s other son, Henry Jones, received a substantial portion of land that would later become part of western Cary. Either he or his father constructed a home around 1803, which eventually came to be known as the Nancy Jones House. This structure would later serve as a focal point for local history, embodying the Jones family's enduring impact on the region.

During the same era, another figure named Nathaniel Jones emerged in the area, complicating local lore. This Nathaniel Jones, unaffiliated with the Crabtree lineage, became known as Nathaniel Jones of White Plains. His nickname derived from his vast cotton fields that, when in bloom, created an expanse resembling white plains. By the time of his death, he had accumulated an impressive ten thousand acres, becoming one of the region's largest landowners.

Nathaniel Jones of White Plains played a prominent role in state and local governance. He served as a Wake County judge, a member of the North Carolina Assembly and a delegate to the state's Constitutional Convention. A fervent Patriot during the American Revolution, he also offered his land as a potential site for the new state capital in 1792. Although his property was one of four finalists, Cary lost by a narrow margin to Raleigh. A persistent legend suggests that Joel Lane, whose land was ultimately chosen, swayed the commissioners with a special drink on the eve of the vote. However, Lane himself was outmaneuvered by other contenders when Cary was proposed as the site for the University of North Carolina, with Chapel Hill eventually prevailing.

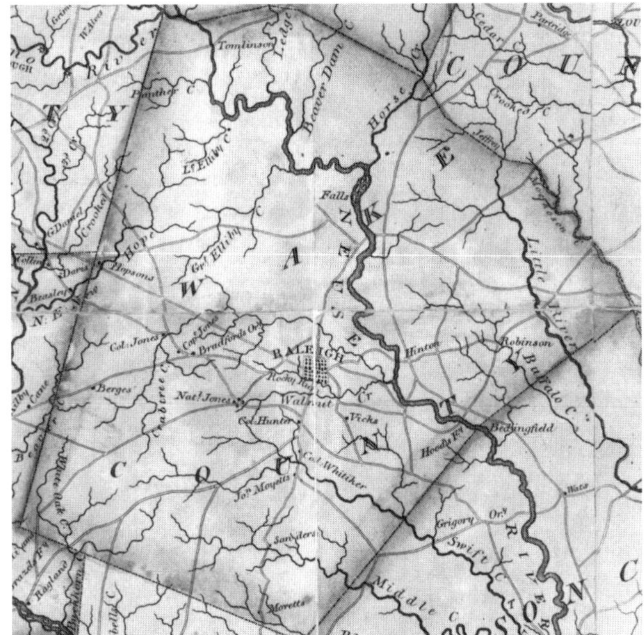

Left: 1808 *Price Strother Map* of the first survey of North Carolina, Wake County portion. *Library of Congress.*

Below: Nathaniel Jones of White Plains homestead. *Elizabeth Reid Murray.*

In 1815, Nathaniel Jones of White Plains made headlines with his controversial final wish. Succumbing to a reported "sore throat," he left a will requesting the emancipation of all his enslaved workers, an extraordinary stance at the time. In his will, he provided a detailed explanation, stating his belief that all humans are entitled to freedom, condemning his conscience for maintaining slavery and adhering to the Golden Rule. However, his

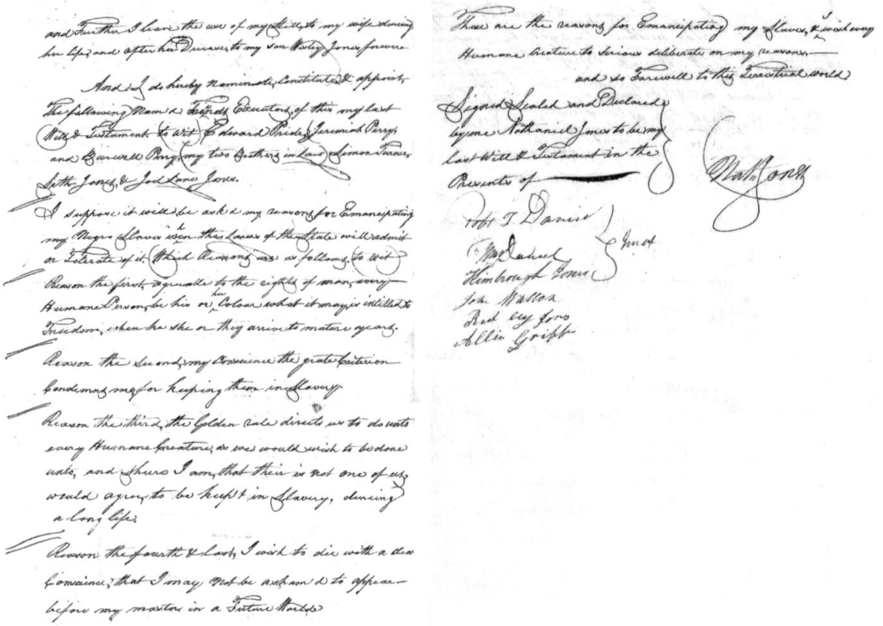

and Further I leave the use of my Still, to my wife during her life, and after her Decease, to my son Wesley Jones forever.

And I do hereby nominate, Constitute & appoint, the following Men & Friends Executors of this my last Will & Testament, to wit, Edward Pride, Jeremiah Perry, and Burwell Perry, (my two Brothers in Law) Simon Turner, Seth Jones, & Joel Lane Jones.

I suppose it will be ask'd my reasons for Emancipating my Negro Slaves when the Laws of the State will admit or Tolerate of it. (Which Reasons are as follows, to wit)

Reason the first, agreeable to the rights of man, every Humane Person, be his or her Colour what it may, is intitled to Freedom, when he she or they arrive to mature years.

Reason the Second, my Conscience the grate Criterion condemns me for keeping them in Slavery.

Reason the third, the Golden rule directs us to do unto every Humane Creature, as we would wish to be done unto, and Shure I am, that their is not one of us would agree to be kept in Slavery, during a long life.

Reason the fourth & last, I wish to die with a clear Conscience, that I may not be asham'd to appear before my master in a Future World.

These are the reasons for Emancipating my Slaves, & I wish every Humane Creature to Serious deliberate on my reasons.—

and so Farewell to this Terrestrial world

Signed Sealed and Declared by me Nathaniel Jones to be my last Will & Testament in the Presents of

Nat. Jones

Robt. T. Daniel
[illegible] Daniel
Kimbrough Jones
John Walton
[illegible]
Allen Griffin
Jurat

Original 1815 will of Nathaniel Jones of White Plains, referencing slave release. *Ancestry.com.*

wishes could not be legally fulfilled, as North Carolina law prohibited the manumission of enslaved individuals. Today, Jones's burial site in the Maynard Oaks subdivision serves as a reminder of his progressive views, at least near the end of his life. Marked by a fifteen-foot obelisk, the family cemetery has been restored and is maintained by the Town of Cary, Asbury Station Chapter of the Daughters of the American Revolution and the Friends of the Page-Walker.

The intertwined stories of Nathaniel Jones of Crabtree and Nathaniel Jones of White Plains became emblematic of the area's rich history. At one point, the two Nathaniels directly competed for a seat in the House of Commons. During the campaign, White Plains made a remark intended as humor but was perceived as an insult, suggesting that Crabtree's supporters couldn't afford shoes and that it was too cold to walk barefooted to Raleigh to vote. The comment galvanized Crabtree's constituents, who, according to a 1900 newspaper article, arrived in Raleigh in droves, barefoot but determined, with their shoes defiantly slung over their shoulders, and secured a decisive victory for their candidate.

Top, left: Original condition of Nathaniel Jones of White Plains' grave site. *Page-Walker Historical Collection*; *Top, right*: Restored Nathaniel Jones of White Plains' grave site in modern-day Cary. *Author's collection*; *Bottom*. Nathaniel Jones of White Plains' cemetery in modern-day Cary neighborhood. *Author's collection.*

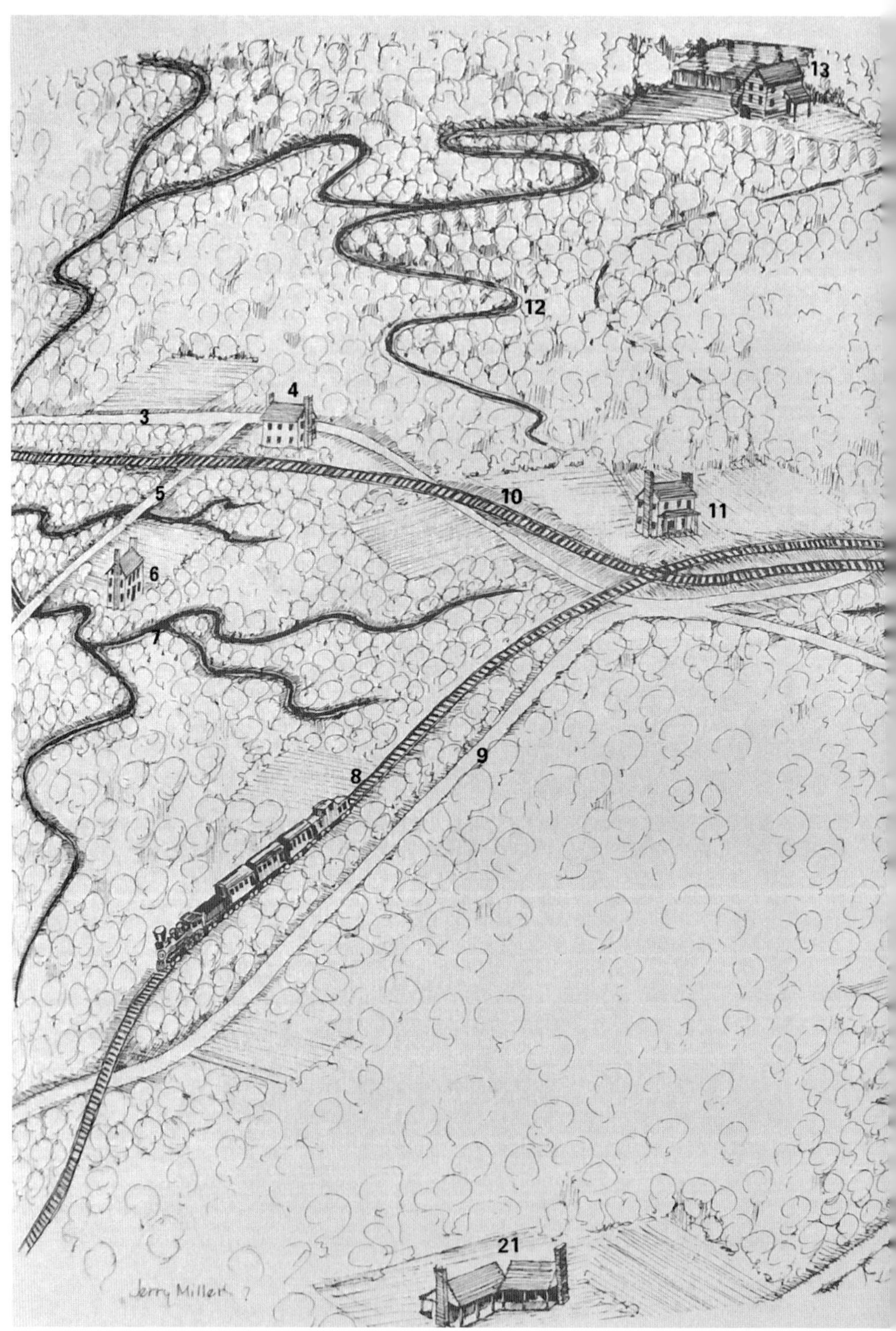

Map of primary structures in the 1800s. *From* Around and About Cary *(original 1971 edition).*

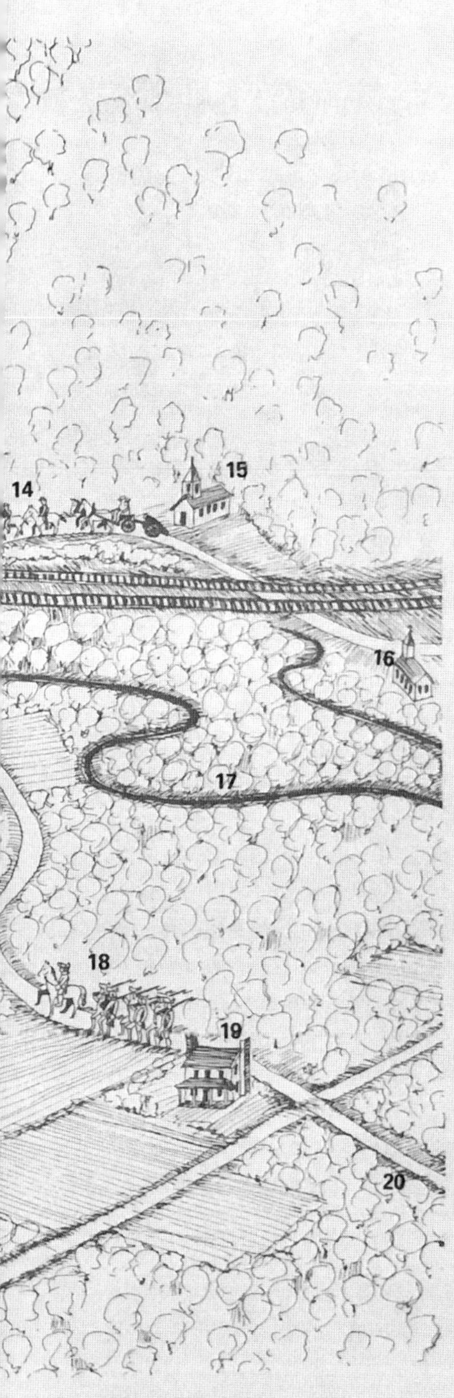

1. Plantation of Colonel Tingnall Jones; now Morrisville.
2. Francis Jones settles on Crabtree Creek, 1749.
3. Hillsborough Road; sometimes called Cornwallis Road.
4. Jones House; setting for legend of two governors; approximate location of early inn and railroad station.
5. Pittsboro Road; built before 1833.
6. High House; home of Fanning Jones, the "old tory."
7. Branches of Crabtree Creek.
8. Chatham Railroad, now Seaboard; built about 1865; activated about 1868.
9. Haywood Road; built before 1808.
10. North Carolina Railroad, now Southern; built through here in 1854.
11. Location of Bradford's Ordinary in 1808; later location of Page House; now center of Cary.
12. Black Creek.
13. Old Company Mill; stood on Crabtree Creek from about 1810 until 1930's.
14. Arrival of General Sherman's Army, 1865.
15. Asbury Meeting House; built early 1800's, approximate location of early railroad station.
16. Ephesus Baptist Church; first built across railroad in 1857.
17. Walnut Creek.
18. Governor Tryon arrives in 1771; creates the legend of Ramsgate (Rhamkette) Road.
19. White Plains Mansion; built before 1808.
20. Road to New Bern.
21. Bennett Place; supposedly begun in 1775.

The rivalry between the two families took a personal turn when Nancy Jones, daughter of Nathaniel Jones of White Plains, married Henry Jones, son of Nathaniel Jones of Crabtree. The couple resided in the 1803 house that became known as the Nancy Jones House. This home became a renowned stagecoach stop, hosting notable figures, including President James K. Polk. Its prominence put Cary on the map as a key waypoint between eastern cities like New Bern and Raleigh and western locales like Hillsborough and Chapel Hill.

Legendary Events at the Historic Nancy Jones House

Nathaniel Jones of White Plains and Nathaniel Jones of Crabtree were not only political rivals but also became in-laws through the marriage of Nancy Jones, the daughter of White Plains, to Henry Jones, the son of Crabtree, in 1813. This union, while significant for its familial and political implications, became intertwined with the legacy of the Nancy Jones House, a site that remains Cary's oldest surviving residential structure and a symbol of its layered history. Nancy's life after Henry's death around 1841 reflects her resilience, as she managed their household and operated an informal stagecoach stop until her passing in 1876.

The Nancy Jones House originally stood at 9391 Chapel Hill Road, a prime location along a key travel route between Raleigh and Chapel Hill. In 2019, the Town of Cary acquired the structure with the intention of preserving its historical significance, as the property beneath it was not owned by the town. By March 2021, the house had been carefully relocated five hundred feet east of its original site to land owned by the town. Despite this move, the house retained its listing in the National Register of Historic Places, a recognition of its enduring historical and architectural value. In June 2023, it also received designation as a local historic landmark, affirming its importance in the cultural heritage of Cary. Preservation efforts are now underway by the town.

The house's historical importance extends beyond its architecture or the union of the two Nathaniel Jones families. It served as a vital stagecoach stop on the Raleigh–Chapel Hill route during the nineteenth century, hosting many of North Carolina's most prominent figures. According to the application for its inclusion in the National Register, the Nancy Jones House welcomed governors, judges, senators and other influential individuals of

Above: The Nancy Jones House in its original location. *University of North Carolina–Chapel Hill, Davis Library, Postcard Collection.*

Left: Nancy Jones. *Page-Walker Historical Collection.*

the era, including President James K. Polk in 1847. These connections underscore the house's role as a hub of political and social activity during its time.

Among its many stories, one of the most famous—despite Cary's later reputation as a dry town—concerns the origin of a well-known bar phrase. While other locations have attempted to claim it, evidence points to the Nancy Jones House as its true birthplace. Historical accounts and family oral histories recount that this phrase was uttered in the parlor of the house during a visit by North Carolina Governor Edward Dudley and South Carolina Governor Pierce Butler in June 1838. As the governors stopped for refreshment during their journey, they were served Nancy Jones's renowned apple and peach brandies. After finishing their drinks, they found the decanters absent, leaving them staring into their empty glasses. Amid the awkward silence, Governor Dudley reportedly exclaimed, "It's a damned long time between drinks!"

This phrase, immortalized in American folklore, has been the subject of considerable research, even drawing the attention of federal investigators. A diary belonging to Nancy Jones, passed down through her granddaughter Carrie Thomas Price, provides a firsthand account of the event. Further corroboration comes from Nancy's grandson Joel Whitaker, who shared the story with the *Raleigh News & Observer* in 1923. While the phrase has achieved global recognition, it remains a proud piece of Cary's local history.

The Nancy Jones House's lore extends beyond political anecdotes to personal and even ghostly tales. Around 1915, the Heater family, who became prominent figures in Cary, lived in the house after moving from West Virginia. Patriarch Russell O. Heater, later known as "Mr. Cary" for his passionate promotion of the town and who will be discussed more later, brought his family to this historic home, where they experienced both its charm and its mysteries. Bob Heater, one of Russell's sons, recounted that his older sister, Margaret, vividly remembered the steady stream of men who rode the rails and sought food from their home. Mrs. Heater, ever hospitable, often provided cornbread to these visitors, although the family kept a sturdy peach limb by the door for protection.

The Heaters also encountered men mistakenly seeking "services" at the house, under the false assumption that it was a brothel. These incidents often ended with Mr. Heater sending the men away and Mrs. Heater slamming the door in their faces. Margaret Heater believed the house to be haunted, frequently hearing unexplained footsteps. One particularly eerie event

Left: Pierce Mason Butler, South Carolina governor, 1836–39. *Town of Edgefield, South Carolina.*

Right: Edward Bishop Dudley, North Carolina governor, 1836–41. *Wikimedia Commons.*

occurred when Aunt Opal, a visiting relative, heard strange noises in the night. Armed with a flashlight and a gun, she investigated the cellar, only to discover what appeared to be blood seeping from the walls. Upon closer inspection, the "blood" turned out to be wine from a long-forgotten cellar of bottles that had exploded over time, possibly remnants of Nancy Jones's famous brandy.

The family's departure from the Nancy Jones House came after Mrs. Heater refused to stay in a home where doors inexplicably unlocked themselves overnight. Subsequent tenants also reported strange occurrences, including phantom footsteps. One frustrated resident reportedly performed a "casting out" ritual to rid the house of its spectral intrusions.

In 2019, the Sri Venkateswara Temple, which owned the land on which the Nancy Jones House stood, sold the property to the Town of Cary with the stipulation that the house be relocated. The move, executed in March 2021, ensured the preservation of this historic structure while accommodating future development. The house's designation in the National Register of Historic Places was successfully maintained, a testament to its enduring significance. Today, the Nancy Jones House remains at its new location on Chapel Hill Road, serving as a tangible connection to Cary's earliest days.

The Nancy Jones House holds a special place in North Carolina's history, not merely as a physical structure but as a symbol of the region's evolution. It represents the blending of two influential families, the development of Cary as a crossroads for travelers and the rich tapestry of lore that continues to fascinate historians and residents alike. Whether as a stagecoach stop hosting presidents and governors or the site of a legendary phrase born in its parlor, the Nancy Jones House endures as a cornerstone of Cary's heritage.

Revolutionary "Cary"

In 1771, William Tryon, the royal governor of North Carolina, set out on a mission to crush a rebellion brewing in the Piedmont region. The Regulators, a group of discontented farmers based around Hillsborough, accused Crown representatives of corruption and refused to pay taxes. Viewing their defiance of King George III's authority as an egregious act of disloyalty, Tryon mobilized one thousand troops to march from New Bern, the capital at the time, to quell the uprising.

Evidence suggests that Tryon's army passed through what is now Cary. On May 7, 1771, part of the army camped overnight at the property of Nathaniel Jones of Crabtree Creek. From there, Tryon and his troops traveled routes that correspond to the modern-day, aptly named Tryon Road, Macedonia Road and Walnut Street, ultimately moving through central Cary en route to Hillsborough. Local lore holds that Tryon either constructed or improved on existing roads to accommodate his troops and artillery, turning Cary into a key link between New Bern and Hillsborough. This strategic path became a vital thoroughfare in colonial North Carolina. The march culminated in the Battle of Alamance, where Tryon secured a decisive victory. Although the battle temporarily restored royal authority, it also foreshadowed the larger conflict of the Revolutionary War.

The High House

Cary's connection to Revolutionary War history deepens with the enigmatic figure of David Fanning, described as "the most perfect scoundrel in the history of the state." David Fanning led a band of Loyalists during the Revolutionary War, famously kidnapping Patriot Governor Thomas Burke and delivering him to British forces. However, confusion persists about whether Fanning had ties to Cary's Fanning Jones, a man linked to the area's storied High House. Both were natives of Wake County, and the shared name raises questions about their relationship.

High House, an iconic structure of Revolutionary War–era Cary, stood near the intersection of High House Road and Northwest Maynard Road on today's Black Creek Greenway. According to Hope Summerell Chamberlain's 1921 historical account, the house was an imposing four-square structure that had already been abandoned and fallen into disrepair by the early twentieth century. Chamberlain's source, a relative of Fanning Jones, recounted how Jones was ostracized by his family and community, referred to as the "Old Tory" and eventually driven from the region. Fanning Jones later relocated to Tennessee, leaving his property to be sold by his lawyer. The High House land eventually passed to Green Alford and, later, the Williams family, who abandoned it in the 1920s. Over time, the house deteriorated, with only its chimney and foundation remaining before those, too, disappeared.

Modern efforts to trace the High House's history gained clarity with the identification of the High House family cemetery. Located near the Black Creek Greenway on private land at the intersection of Darbytown Place and Buckland Mills Court, the cemetery, now known as the Stedman Family Cemetery, was rediscovered in 2003 during neighborhood development. Developer Michael Dean Chadwick uncovered at least eighteen graves, some predating the 1820s to 1860s inscriptions on existing markers. To preserve the site's historical integrity, Chadwick built around the cemetery rather than relocating the graves.

The High House is steeped in legends, including tales of hauntings and hidden treasure. One such story involves Leander Williams, a former resident born in the 1880s. After moving away, Leander had a vivid dream of buried treasure beneath the fireplace hearth of the old house. Remarkably, his mother reported having the same dream. Rushing back to investigate, they discovered that someone had already recently dismantled the hearth, leaving the mystery of the supposed buried treasure unresolved. While there is no

Entrance to the Black Creek Greenway, former location of the High House. *Author's collection.*

THE WORD FROM | CARY'S HUGGINS GLEN

Despite building plans, graves will rest in peace

By Lorenzo Perez
STAFF WRITER

CARY – Some of the sunken patches in this wooded area could be natural indentations in the rolling terrain.

The scattering of crumbling headstones suggests otherwise, however. Orange flags now mark the 18 confirmed grave sites detected off the 500 block of High House Road.

They date to the late 1800s, and they rest in the middle of what's supposed to be Huggins Glen, a planned-unit development of $300,000 homes.

It's still not uncommon for developers in Wake County to stumble across old, abandoned graves. When possible, the remains are removed and reinterred elsewhere.

That was considered in this case. But with 18 graves and possibly more still undetected, 1st American developer Michael Dean Chadwick says it's better to build around them and let Mary D. Stedman, William A. Stedman, Adail Stedman and the others buried there rest in peace.

So the graves will remain, secure in a 3,500-square-foot lot potentially surrounded by new houses.

The gravestone for William Stedman leans against a tree in an old cemetery in Cary. A developer planning a subdivision found the cemetery and plans to build around it.

STAFF PHOTO BY SCOTT SHARPE

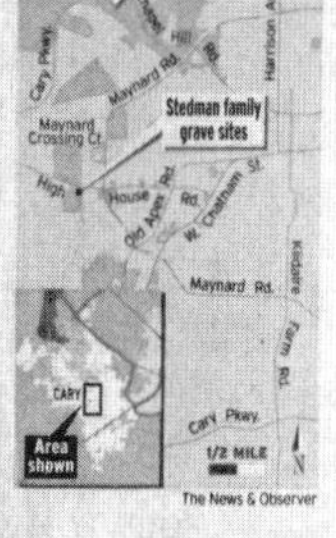

The News & Observer

The years have worn what's left of the headstones almost smooth, and lichen covers many of the dates.

The top of Mary D. Stedman's grave reads "Borned Feb. 24, 1829." She was the wife of J.B. Stedman, who was one of three men who helped form Cary Township's first public school committee after the Civil War, according to "Around and About Cary," an unofficial history of the town written by Thomas M. Byrd. A distant descendant of the Stedman family has been contacted in Sea Island, Ga., Chadwick says, but little else is known about who is buried in the sunken graves.

Unrolling a map showing the layout of the proposed development, the 50-year-old Apex developer says he's glad they were able to preserve the graves. The 22 acres rest right off of a busy stretch of High House Road, and the whoosh of morning commuters driving past intrudes on the quiet inside the wooded area.

"This is really a killer site," Chadwick says. "This is the kind of place I could move to myself."

Staff writer Lorenzo Perez can be reached at 829-8937 or lperez@newsobserver.com.

Developer discovers High House family cemetery. *From the* News and Observer, *March 25, 2003.*

Above: High House family cemetery today on private land in Cary neighborhood. *Author's collection.*

Left: High House circa 1897. Pictured are members of the Nathaniel Green Williams family and one courting beau in the horse and buggy. *Mark Williams.*

proof that treasure existed, the hearth played a documented role during the Civil War. Susan Alford Adams, a descendant of Nathaniel Green Alford, recounted how valuables were hidden under a removable stone in the hearth as General Sherman's troops approached. An enslaved man named Uncle Dave feigned illness by standing on the spot, successfully deterring soldiers from inspecting it. Sherman's troops refrained from occupying the house, allowing the family's valuables to remain safe.

In addition to its mysterious tales, the High House property holds an enduring legacy through its historical significance. Although the house itself is gone, its lore continues to intrigue historians and residents alike.

Cary's Only Known Revolutionary War Patriot Grave

The Revolutionary War era also left its mark on another prominent figure associated with Cary: Nathaniel Jones of White Plains. As mentioned previously, Jones of White Plains, father of Nancy Jones, was a staunch Patriot who offered his land as a potential site for North Carolina's capital following the war, although his bid failed. His estate spanned more than ten thousand acres in what is now eastern Cary, and his burial site remains one of the town's most significant hidden landmarks. Located in the cul-de-sac of Tolliver Court in Maynard Oaks, the Nathaniel Jones family cemetery includes a tall obelisk marking Jones's grave and a plaque from the Daughters of the American Revolution recognizing him as a Revolutionary War veteran. This cemetery, likely dating back to the 1780s, stands as a testament to Cary's deep roots in early American history.

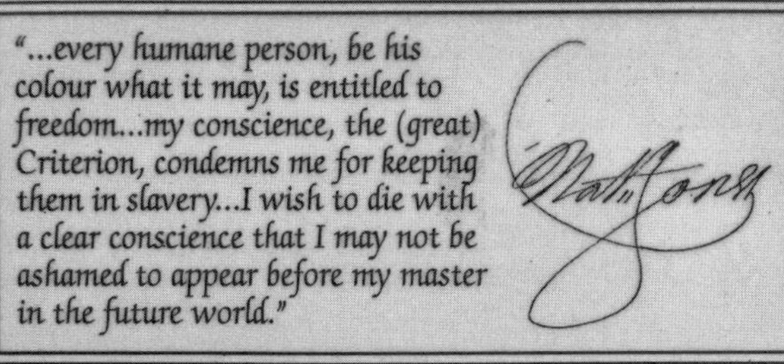

Historical sign posted at Nathaniel Jones of White Plains' cemetery. *Author's collection.*

TWO NEAR MISSES

The Revolutionary War era also left its mark on Cary's history with intriguing "almosts"—or near misses, depending on your perspective. These are moments when Cary's destiny teetered on the edge of significant transformation and defining moments in the future of the town. One of these pivotal episodes involved Nathaniel Jones of White Plains. After the Revolutionary War, North Carolina sought a new capital to replace New Bern, which had been compromised during British occupation. In March 1792, ten state-appointed commissioners were tasked with selecting one thousand acres within ten miles of Isaac Hunter's Tavern in Wake County. Among the tracts considered on March 21, 1792, was one owned by Nathaniel Jones, situated near what is now Walnut Street in Cary. Out of seventeen sites reviewed, only four garnered votes, and Jones's land was among them. However, subsequent rounds of voting favored Joel Lane's property in what would become Raleigh. According to local lore, Lane's hospitality—enhanced by his homemade apple brandy—may have influenced the commissioners' decision. It's fascinating to imagine that Cary High School could have been the site of North Carolina's state capitol if events had unfolded differently.

Joel Lane's connection to Cary extended beyond his successful bid for the capital. He also owned land in the area, offering part of it as a potential site for the University of North Carolina. This land, believed to be near the intersection of today's East Chatham Street and Reedy Creek Road, was seriously considered before Chapel Hill was ultimately chosen. The decision ensured that the university would not bear the name "University of North Carolina at Cary."

While Cary missed out on hosting the state's capital and its flagship university, these near misses shaped its identity and future. The town's proximity to Raleigh and Chapel Hill afforded it unique opportunities, fostering growth and connecting it to the institutions of state governance and higher education. Cary's early role as the "place in between" became a defining characteristic, laying the groundwork for its evolution into a thriving community positioned between historical significance and modern progress.

By the early nineteenth century, Cary's role in the region had evolved. Its designation as the "place in between" arose from its location halfway between Raleigh and points west. This positioning gained importance with two key developments. First, the construction of the Nancy Jones

House around 1803 established Cary as a waypoint. Second, the arrival of the North Carolina Railroad in 1852 solidified its status as a critical hub in the growing network of transportation and trade. Together, these milestones shaped Cary's transformation from a sleepy colonial outpost into a burgeoning community.

Today, Cary's Revolutionary War history remains a rich tapestry of fact and folklore. The stories of Nathaniel Jones of White Plains, High House and Governor Tryon's march through the area serve as reminders of the town's vital role in shaping North Carolina's early identity. Through preservation and storytelling, these connections to the past continue to resonate, offering a glimpse into the challenges and triumphs of those who once called this land home.

ENTER FRANK PAGE...
AND THE CIVIL WAR

Allison Francis "Frank" Page, the founder of Cary, North Carolina, was a man of significant stature—both physically and figuratively. Standing over six feet tall, which was uncommon for his time, Frank commanded attention with his imposing presence. His well-groomed beard and strong, self-made demeanor added to his larger-than-life reputation. Frank was not only physically impressive but also renowned for his pioneering spirit, adventurous nature and a reputation for speaking his mind when others were too hesitant to voice their opinions. His values were deeply rooted in five key principles: God, family, temperance, education and entrepreneurship. To imagine Frank in a modern context, think of the Brawny paper towels man—a robust, dependable figure, ready to take on whatever challenges came his way.

Born in 1824 to a respected farming family in what is now the Leesville area of Wake County, Frank grew up as one of ten children. His family ensured that all their children received a college education, but Frank himself did not attend college. Instead, he became a self-made entrepreneur at the age of sixteen. Frank won a contract to supply lumber for the Raleigh and Gaston Railroad, an endeavor that took him to Fayetteville, where he worked to harvest lumber. While there, he earned a reputation for his ingenuity when he crafted a raft from freshly cut logs and ferried himself down the Cape Fear River—a testament to his resourcefulness and adventurous nature.

It was during this time that Frank met his future wife, Catherine Frances "Kate" Raboteau. Some accounts suggest that Kate first saw Frank as he

Left: Allison Francis "Frank" Page. *From* The Life and Times of Walter Hines Page, *vol. 1, 1925.*

Right: Catherine "Kate" Raboteau Page. *From* The Life and Times of Walter Hines Page, *vol. 1, 1925.*

ferried his lumber down the river, an image that likely captured her attention. Born in 1831, Kate came from a well-to-do family with French Huguenot roots. She was highly educated, excelling in French, algebra and literature, making her education and intellectualism a sharp contrast to Frank's more practical, self-taught background. However, despite these differences, they shared a deep connection built on common values of faith, integrity and a strong sense of personal accomplishment. Their relationship flourished, marked by mutual respect, love, humor and a professional partnership that would sustain them.

In 1849, when Kate was seventeen and Frank was twenty-four, they married and purchased 218 acres of land near Kate's family, where they began farming. By 1854, they had made the decision to move to a new piece of land that would later become Cary. While the exact reasons for this move remain unclear, Frank's pioneering spirit and the potential opportunity presented by the North Carolina Railroad's expansion likely played a significant role. In 1854, the railroad was building tracks from Raleigh to Hillsborough, passing through what is now downtown Cary. The land also offered an abundance of prime timber, which Frank, with his background

Frank Page homestead in Cary, mid-1850s. *Page-Walker Historical Collection.*

in lumber, must have seen as a valuable resource. They purchased 300 acres for seven dollars per acre and set about building their home on the site of Bradford's Ordinary, a 1760 saloon and inn, located where Cary Town Hall now stands.

Despite the irony of choosing to build their home on a site that had once been a tavern—especially given Frank and Kate's ardent commitment to temperance—the couple was determined to make the best of it. In the mid-1800s, building a structure from scratch was no small feat. It was common for people to repurpose existing buildings and foundations to save time and money. Frank and Kate surely worked to cleanse the space of its previous use, both physically and spiritually, creating a home that would serve as the foundation for their future.

WHEN THE WHISTLE BLOWS DURING THE CIVIL WAR

Despite Frank's early efforts to build the little village near the railroad tracks, the train didn't stop in the village that would become Cary.

Ironically, Frank got his wish during the Civil War, but for all the wrong reasons. When the train whistle blew during the Civil War, it meant the

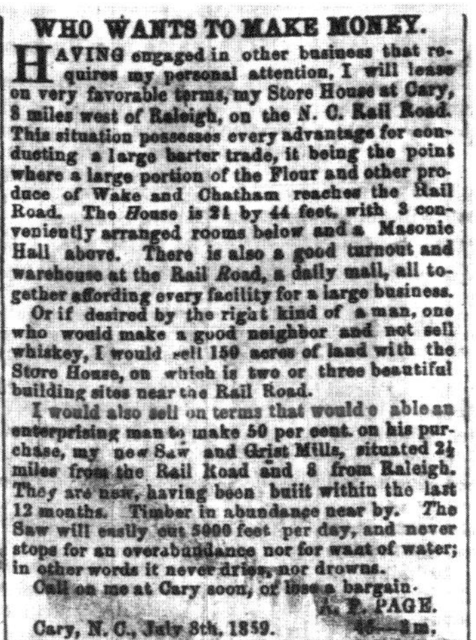

WHO WANTS TO MAKE MONEY.

HAVING engaged in other business that requires my personal attention, I will lease on very favorable terms, my Store House at Cary, 8 miles west of Raleigh, on the N. C. Rail Road. This situation possesses every advantage for conducting a large barter trade, it being the point where a large portion of the Flour and other produce of Wake and Chatham reaches the Rail Road. The House is 24 by 44 feet, with 3 conveniently arranged rooms below and a Masonic Hall above. There is also a good turnout and warehouse at the Rail Road, a daily mail, all together affording every facility for a large business.

Or if desired by the right kind of a man, one who would make a good neighbor and not sell whiskey, I would sell 150 acres of land with the Store House, on which is two or three beautiful building sites near the Rail Road.

I would also sell on terms that would enable an enterprising man to make 50 per cent. on his purchase, my new Saw and Grist Mills, situated 2½ miles from the Rail Road and 8 from Raleigh. They are new, having been built within the last 12 months. Timber in abundance near by. The Saw will easily cut 5000 feet per day, and never stops for an overabundance nor for want of water; in other words it never dries, nor drowns.

Call on me at Cary soon, or lose a bargain.

A. F. PAGE.

Cary, N. C., July 8th, 1859. [illegible]

Frank Page marketing the land that would be Cary. *From* Spirit of the Age, *July 20, 1859.*

train would stop in the village, but only to offload the body of a local who had died in the conflict. When the villagers would hear the whistle, they would all rush to the unofficial train stop, which was right in front of the Page Homestead, approximately where downtown railroad crossing is today on Academy Street. They would rush there in an absolute panic because it was only when the simple coffin was offloaded from the train and the deceased's name could be read on the side that the families would know which of them would have their lives changed forever due to the loss of a son or father.

Frank would join the villagers in these moments, not only as the village's unofficial leader but also as the area's railroad agent, to meet the train and console the waiting villagers and ultimately offer support to the grieving family. It is during the Civil War that the area was first called Page's Turnout or Page's Station—a name created by consensus and word of mouth for the man who was championing the area forward, rather than official naming.

SHERMAN'S SECRET PLAN HATCHED IN CARY

Frank, who saw the Civil War as a "foolish enterprise," was deeply affected by the events of the conflict. His home, along with the nearby Nancy Jones House, was occupied by Union soldiers. Kate and their four young children at the time were forced to live upstairs while Union officers took over the first floor. With Frank's businesses mostly in ruins and the village struggling, the family relied on their orchard, which produced peaches that Frank sold to the Union troops, for their livelihood. In fact, it was reported that most of the Page family income came from the sale of these peaches during the war.

The impact of the war was far-reaching, and in 1865, when the war was drawing to a close, Page's Station became home to 1,700 Union soldiers under the command of General Frances Preston Blair Jr. The village's

Left: General Francis Preston Blair Jr., Union major general in the Civil War. *Library of Congress.*

Right: Commanding General of the Union army William T. Sherman. *National Archives and Records Administration.*

Opposite: Poem on Lincoln's assassination written at Page's Turnout. *From the* Daily Standard, *April 19, 1865.*

strategic location between Raleigh and Bennett Place—where General Sherman would eventually meet with General Johnston to negotiate the surrender of Confederate forces in North Carolina—would prove to be significant in the final days of the war. On April 15, 1865, as General Sherman was traveling by train to Bennett Place, he received news that President Abraham Lincoln had been assassinated. He made an unexpected stop at Page's Station, where he met with General Blair and shared the tragic news. Sherman ordered that the news be kept secret from the Union troops to prevent any potential reprisals or escalation of the conflict.

Sherman's decision to keep the news from the troops was partly due to his belief that North Carolina was still divided on the issue of secession, having been the second to last state to leave the Union. Additionally, Blair held a special place in his heart for the area, being a graduate of the University of North Carolina. Sherman and Blair agreed that the information would not be shared with the soldiers. After Sherman continued his successful journey to Bennett Place to negotiate surrender,

For the Standard.

On President Lincoln's Death.

BY R. M.

Lincoln, our noble President, is dead!
Dead—let the nation mourn.
Eternal glories cluster round his head,
For him 'tis glory's morn.

Our glorious President is gone, for aye,
Killed by a murderer's hand;
His blessed spirit shines in heaven's bright day,
While sorrow fills the land.

Oh! doubly cruel was the traitorous lead,
And doubly bright the blood,
That left his heart while his pure spirit fled
To its final rest with God.

What honored title shall his memory crown?
What monument be built
To tell to other worlds his great renown,
And his assassin's guilt?

His monumental stone is in our souls,
His memory's sacred shrine,
Shall last while the eternal ocean rolls
Mingling with the divine.

Page's Station, N. C., April 17, 1865.

Lincoln's assassination was officially shared with the Union troops. Although it caused a stir among the Union soldiers at the occupied Page homestead—including an anecdotal report of Kate being confronted by a Union soldier exclaiming, "You have played hell now, Mrs. Page"—Sherman's orders, along with Blair's support, ensured that the situation did not escalate into further violence.

A Union soldier, upon learning about the assassination, composed a tribute poem at the Page homesite. The poem was later published in newspapers nationwide. This poem is significant in establishing the historical events at the site, as the author explicitly noted that it was written at Page's Station, one of the early names for what is now modern-day Cary, specifically located at today's town hall location, where the Page homestead stood and a Union occupation occurred.

THE MASONS

Regardless of the mercy shown in the end of the Civil War, the area that would be called Cary was still devastated. Many local leaders stepped forward to help support widows and children after the war, reestablish crops and grow local business. The local Masons, of which Frank Page was a founding member, were very active in these efforts.

Like in many southern towns, the Masons provided leadership and charity to families after the Civil War. The Masons established in the area in 1858 as Lodge No. 198, thirteen years before the Cary's incorporation. Notably,

Opposite: Modern-day Ashworth building at Christmas. *Heather Leah.*

Above: Cary Masonic Lodge plaque. *Author's collection.*

Right: Original Cary Masonic Lodge staircase. *Author's collection.*

their charter reveals one of the earliest recorded uses of the name "Cary" in the small village. In the absence of a formal town structure, churches or civic organizations, the Masonic Lodge played a vital role in guiding the village. However, due to the Masons' secret operations and practices, much of that leadership happened behind the scenes.

During the Civil War, the Masons served as a singular source of support for the community. Amid heightened membership and active charitable endeavors, the Masons leveraged its influence and resources to provide crucial aid to families in need. Records show that Frank Page, despite facing personal bankruptcy and occupation of his home during the war, made a financial donation through the Lodge for war widows and orphans.

The Masonic Lodge became a home for local leaders, many of whom would later serve as mayors or hold other prominent positions in Cary's future. Between 1870 and 1931, the Lodge met in a structure positioned at the junction of Chatham and Academy Streets. In 1931, the Cary Masons undertook the construction of the town's tallest building of its era on the site then known as Uncle Bob's Corner, after the owner and fellow Mason, Robert Harrison. The ground floor was designated for commerce and eventually a pharmacy, while the Masons convened on the second floor, granting them a panoramic view of Cary. This historic establishment, now known as the Ashworth building, remains to this day with the second floor still featuring original floors and other remnants from its Masonic Lodge days.

The Masonic symbol can be seen on the Ashworth Building on the second-floor exterior facing Academy Street, and the Masonic cornerstone is located at the corner of Academy and Chatham Streets. The blue staircase connecting the street to the second-floor Lodge remains in its original condition, bearing witness to more than one hundred years of Cary's history as local leaders ascended its steps. Today, the Cary Masonic Lodge meets on Maynard Road.

PAGE'S RESILIENCE AFTER THE CIVIL WAR

After the Civil War, Frank Page was bankrupt, and his village was suffering. But Frank was resourceful, as was his wife, Kate. Mrs. Page was ready to restore her occupied house back into a home for her family. The first floor of the Page homestead had been transformed into a military outpost during the war. Valuables had been taken, furniture had been destroyed and curtains had been removed to provide unobstructed vantage points. A household budget was nonexistent for Kate to rebuild. Frank's businesses had gone under, and selling peaches from the orchard, no matter how wonderful they tasted, only went so far. Besides being intelligent and resourceful, Kate reportedly had a keen sense of humor. So she simply creatively repurposed what she had. To the ironic amusement of her observing family, Kate made house curtains out of the now worthless $100 Confederate currency lying around the house as a first step to start rebuilding a sense of home.

Frank was also determined for him and his little village to make a comeback. He invested in rebuilding his wealth alongside the development of the village. This resulted in Cary's first (of many) land valuation booms in which property he originally bought for $7 per acre was selling in the late 1860s for $200 per acre. For his efforts and leadership, he won a seat in the North Carolina General Assembly after the Civil War in November 1865.

Becoming Cary and Celebrating the Centennial

On April 3, 1871, the General Assembly of North Carolina passed an act to incorporate Cary—putting an errant *e* in the documents by clerical error. It was corrected in later amendments to the town charter, but not before creating much confusion and misprints on early maps—some calling it Page's Turnout or Page's Station, while others naming it Carey. Even after 1900, at the same railroad station, Cary was spelled both Cary and Carey depending on the railroad carrier. The person for whom Cary is named, Samuel Fenton Cary, never used an *e* in his surname.

In Cary's original charter, founder Allison Francis "Frank" Page was named the town's first mayor. He defined Cary's limits as extending a half mile in every direction—about one square mile—from what is now the downtown railroad crossing on Academy Street. The charter also banned alcohol, alcohol licenses and "tippling houses" within Cary and for two miles beyond its limits. Newspapers reported that Frank wanted the ban to last one thousand years, but state lawyers advised him that he could not include a specific time period in the document.

Although the town being referred to as "Cary" appear in the local Masonic chapter's records long before Cary's official founding, it was Frank, who was a founding Mason, who ultimately pushed for the name. Residents of the village were surprised that he would not name the town for himself, but Frank stood firm on his name choice.

Samuel Fenton Cary was a national temperance leader, politician and Civil War general from Cincinnati, Ohio. Yes, Cary is named for a

144 1870–'71.—Chapter 80—81.

and such shall be subject to the general laws upon towns in the revised code, III, and elsewhere, so far as the name may be now in force, and except so far as varied by this charter.

Corporate limits. Sec. 2. That the limits of said town shall be lines running at the distance of one-half mile from the warehouse of the Chatham railroad company in said town, and parallel with the four walls thereof.

Retailing liquor forbidden. Sec. 3. That any licenses to retail spirituous liquor, wine or cordial at Carey, or within two miles thereof, shall be void, and no person shall erect, keep, maintain, or have at Carey or within two miles thereof any tippling house, establishment or place for the sale of wines, cordials, spirituous or malt liquors.

Commissioners. Sec. 4. That the commissioners of said town shall be five in number, and that until their successors shall be elected under the laws of the state, the following persons, viz: R. H. Jones, A. H. Merritt, M. P. Mallett, H. B. Jordan and W. H. Bobbitt, shall be commissioners, and A. F. Page shall be mayor of said town, with all the powers by law conferred upon such officers. Mayor.

When act to be in force. Sec. 5. That this act shall be in force from and after its ratification.

Ratified the 3d day of April, A. D. 1871.

Left: Town of Cary charter in 1871. *Digital NC.*

Right: Samuel Fenton Cary. *Cincinnati Historical Society.*

Union soldier Yankee. He believed that alcohol was an evil that destroyed families, lives and economies and should be outlawed by the government. Starting as a lawyer in his own private law practice, making him wealthy at an early age, he abandoned his law practice in 1884 to dedicate himself full time to the temperance movement. Newspaper articles from the time indicated Cary's reasons for his devotion to temperance: he was a recovering alcoholic himself, and in his experience from his legal practice, the large majority of cases he represented involved alcohol, which led to deleterious outcomes of criminal activity and law enforcement involvement. In 1848, he was elected head of the National Division of the Sons of Temperance, which made him the national leader of the temperance movement.

General Cary came to speak in Raleigh on a few occasions around 1871, and recent historical discoveries indicate he came to visit his namesake during one of those visits. In fact, one interesting newspaper account in the *Raleigh Daily Sentinel* on June 6, 1873, reported that a gentleman representing the flourishing village six miles west of Raleigh offered General Cary a substantial house and lot if he would "renounce his allegiance to Ohio and file his petition for naturalization in North Carolina and take his abode in Cary." General Cary reportedly declined the offer, being a current candidate for governor in Ohio. Few doubt that it was Frank who made this offer.

Designing the Village

Frank's influence enabled him to focus on designing the village layout with an eye toward future growth. His downtown district design, which remains largely intact today, reflected his core values of entrepreneurship, education and religion. To start, Frank engaged surveyors to evaluate the topography of today's downtown, with the goal of identifying the highest point in the village. After careful analysis, it was determined that the land where the Cary Arts Center and Cary Elementary School now stand held this distinction. Recognizing the importance of education and its central role in the community's development, Frank decided to donate this prime land for the construction of a school.

The location of the school held additional significance, as it happened to align almost perfectly with a direct route to Frank's own homestead. Along this path, he envisioned the establishment of churches, emphasizing the importance of religion as a cornerstone of the community. The alignment of these institutions—Frank's homestead, the school and the churches—helped to define what would become a central and enduring thoroughfare for the village. Today, that road is known as Academy Street, a name that reflects Cary's historical prioritization of education.

In Frank's design, commerce and industry were strategically placed to ensure the village's economic vitality. The area designated for commerce was centered along Chatham Street, positioning it as the commercial heart of the village where businesses could thrive and residents could access goods and services. Meanwhile, the industrial sector was situated along Railroad

Opposite: Family and staff at Hobby's Grocery on West Chatham Street. *Page-Walker Arts and History Center/Leslie Douglas.*

This page, top: Chatham Street businesses, with the Ivey-Ellington House. *Page-Walker Arts and History Center/Leslie Douglas.*

This page, bottom: Ashworth's Drug Store, 1970s. *Page-Walker Arts and History Center/Leslie Douglas.*

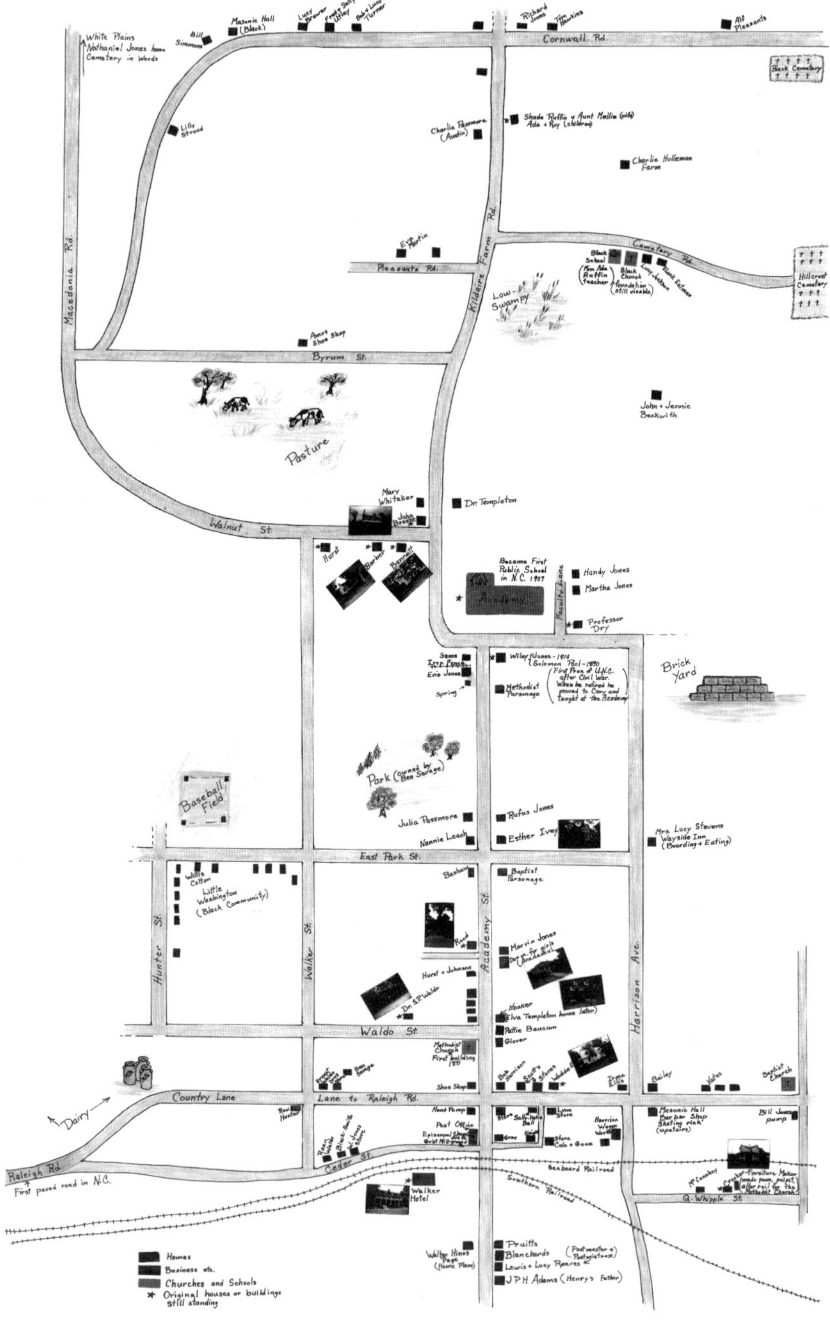

Hand-drawn map of early 1900s Cary, drawn by Anita Richmond with direction from Elva Templeton based on her recollections. *Cary United Methodist Church.*

Street, which is now known as Cedar Street. This location took advantage of the proximity to the railroad, enabling efficient transportation of goods and materials and facilitating industrial growth.

Frank's efforts to organize and structure the village were further supported by the collective action of Cary's residents. About one year after these foundational developments, in August 1872, influential members of the Cary area community—including both white and African American residents—came together to advocate for formal recognition of their growing village. They signed and submitted a petition for the establishment of a new township, demonstrating a shared vision for Cary's future and a commitment to self-governance.

Frank not only designed the physical layout of Cary but also set forth the guiding principles that would shape its future growth. His vision remains evident today. Standing on the steps of the Cary Arts Center—formerly the site of Cary's historic school—you can look straight down Academy Street toward the railroad crossing and the location of Frank's original homestead, which is now town hall. This enduring alignment highlights the lasting influence of Frank's 1871 town design, a framework that continues to define the heart of Cary.

CARY'S CENTENNIAL

Cary's centennial celebration in 1971 marked the town's biggest and most spectacular event in its history. The preparations for the centennial began several years before, with the founding of the Cary Area Centennial Corporation. The corporation, led by then Mayor Veasey, was tasked with overseeing the town's 100th birthday festivities. A budget of $6,000, raised through the sale of centennial bonds, was allocated for the event. To serve as a base of operations, a 384-square-foot centennial headquarters building was constructed, which was later relocated and repurposed as Cary's first chamber of commerce.

Cary's centennial celebration seal. *Digital NC.*

One of the most striking features of Cary's centennial celebration was the formation of 95 local various chapters designed to embody the town's spirit. These chapters included the Centennial Belles, Brothers of the Brush, Little

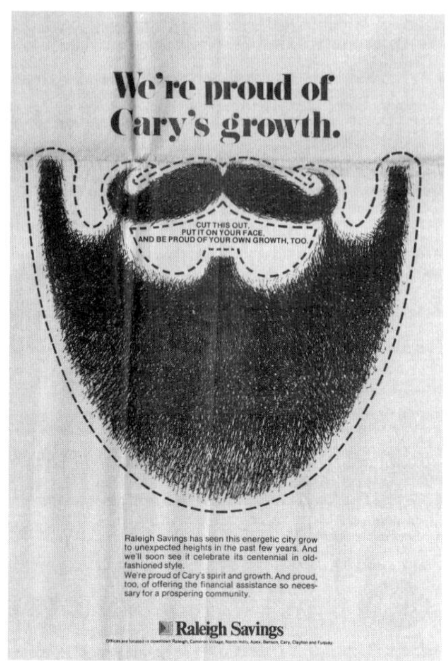

Left: Poster from Cary's centennial celebration in 1971. *Christopher S. Ashworth, Facebook page.*

Right: Raleigh bank advertisement for Cary's centennial celebration. *From the* News and Observer, *April 18, 1971.*

Miss Belles and Little Shavers. In an effort to immerse residents in the era of Cary's founding, men were required to grow beards or face a fine, while women and their families dressed in handmade costumes from 1871. These period costumes were not just for special occasions, but were to be worn everywhere—work, school, church and socially—throughout Centennial Week, which ran from May 8 to May 12. Women wore pins identifying which chapter they belonged to, while men displayed pins denoting their beard status or exemption.

While the costumes were widely embraced, some of Mayor Veasey's other requests were less successful. He asked women to refrain from wearing makeup, nail polish, perfume, jewelry or dyeing their hair to stay true to the 1871 era. They refused.

Several other activities were part of the centennial festivities, including the creation of a Cary Centennial seal, the striking of commemorative souvenir coins and the publication of a commemorative book. In a playful display of community spirit, Cary residents, dressed in their historical garb,

Brothers of the Brush

Cary North Carolina

Celebrating the 100th Anniversary of Cary

This is to certify that I, ____________, being a good civic-minded citizen or resident of the greater Cary area, do hereby agree to do my civic duty and grow a mustache, full beard, goatee, or sideburns as a part of the Centennial Celebration, thus making me a member in good standing of the great society known as the Brothers of the Brush. In the desire to be a booster for the Centennial Celebration, May 7 through May 12, 1971. The above member agrees to wear an official badge and to wear a derby or top hat before and/or during the Celebration days, to take part in Caravan Booster Trips or other activities as directed by the Cary Centennial Committee.

Chairman
Brothers of the Brush

Bob Cassell
Chairman
Participation Division

1871 1971

Award certificate from Cary's centennial celebration. *Digital NC.*

caravanned to neighboring towns, parading down main streets while honking their horns to celebrate Cary's centennial. These spirited excursions were generally good-naturedly received, often with the mayor of the town with other residents meeting the caravan with refreshment.

Centennial Week officially kicked off with a grand hour-and-a-half parade, which was followed by a nightly performance of *The Unbeatable Century*, an original production of Cary history at Cooper Field. Other activities included beard judging contests, where categories ranged from the youngest beard grower to the best and worst beards. There were even kangaroo courts set up in downtown where elected officials and other residents were randomly "imprisoned" in homemade jails for humorous and absurd reasons. In a nod to the past, Cary's local stores even rolled back their prices to thosc from 1871 for the duration of Centennial Week.

Never before, and never since, has Cary celebrated itself with such unity and enthusiasm. The event became a powerful demonstration of community pride and spirit. However, there were some glitches to the festivities besides the women refusing the mayor's order banning makeup and hair dye.

A time capsule was buried on May 12, 1971, in front of Cary's newly constructed federal building at 205 South Academy Street. The capsule contained various documents and mementos from Cary in 1971, including a letter from Mayor Fred Bond to the future mayor of Cary, who would open the capsule in 2071. Mayor Bond was new to office, sworn in only six days prior to Centennial Week—in his 1871 full attire it should be noted. He feared that the 2071 mayor would perceive him as scxist, as Mayor Bond in his first draft of the letter addressed his 2071 successor as "Sir." Realizing

Top: Beard contest winner from Cary's centennial celebration in 1971. *Digital NC.*

Bottom: Cary's Centennial Executive Committee. *From Cary's 100th anniversary commemorative book, 1971.*

that the future mayor could very well be a woman, he rewrote the letter, addressing it to "My Dear Mayor."

The time capsule saga continued, however. In January 1984, after the federal building post office had stood vacant for several years, town officials decided to move the time capsule to a new location beneath the flagpole at the town hall. When the capsule was unearthed, officials were surprised to find it waterlogged, despite it being designed to withstand the elements for one hundred years. Although the capsule was reburied, town officials had second thoughts and dug it up again in September 1984. Upon opening it, they discovered another mess of water-damaged contents. The salvageable items were preserved, while the ruined ones were replaced as much as possible. The items were then placed in a hermetically sealed vault before being reburied, along with a letter explaining the time capsule's tumultuous history at town hall.

The town's 100th birthday became a defining moment in its history, a testament to community pride, creativity and the spirit of celebration alive and well in Cary at that time.

Frank's Lasting Mysteries

Construction Mysteries of the Page-Walker Hotel

Frank was ready to really grow his new town's economy. A top priority was building a railroad hotel to not only encourage the train to stop over in Cary but also as symbolic of the growth of Cary from a village to a town.

It is a commonly accepted narrative that the Page-Walker Hotel was built as Cary's first hotel around 1868 as a railroad hotel. However, a deeper dive into archival records and insights from other Cary historical researchers reveals intriguing questions and inconsistencies that challenge this timeline. By piecing together evidence from directories, newspaper articles and contextual analysis, a more nuanced story emerges about Cary's early hotels, the structures that housed them and the development of the town itself.

The earliest recorded reference to a hotel in Cary comes from *Branson's North Carolina Business Directory of 1869*, which lists "Hotel, Cary, A.F. Page" among the town's businesses. This was a significant milestone, as the earlier 1867 edition of the directory made no mention of a hotel. Instead, the 1867 edition confirmed Frank Page's presence in Cary, noting that he operated a dry goods store and a steam-powered sawmill. It also documented his active role in the Masonic Lodge, where he served as secretary.

This 1869 listing strongly suggests that Frank Page had established a hotel in Cary by that time. However, contemporary searches of newspapers and other archival sources have yielded no corroborating evidence of this hotel in independent reports. The absence of additional documentation raises questions about the nature and significance of the "hotel" mentioned in the directory. It is possible that this was a modest structure—a simple lodging house that did not command the attention of journalists or chroniclers of the era.

By 1871, Cary had been officially incorporated as a town (on April 3, 1871), marking a turning point in its development. An article dated June 8, 1871, provided a glimpse into the town's growth, mentioning plans for the construction of a factory building and a three-story hotel. Both projects were eventually realized, although the exact timeline and sequence of their completion remain unclear.

Descriptions of Cary in 1871 paint a picture of a small community with twenty-five houses, a sash and blind factory, three store buildings (likely including railroad warehouses), Cary Academy and various workshops. All these structures were likely constructed of wood, and there is no mention of a hotel. This omission raises further questions about the 1869 hotel reference. Was it no longer in use by 1871, or was it simply too modest to warrant mention?

Notably, the June 8, 1871 article states that Frank Page planned to build a three-story hotel along with other structures. The wording implies that the envisioned brick hotel had not yet been built. This aligns with later evidence suggesting that the substantial, long-lasting hotel referenced in Cary's history—the structure known today as the Page-Walker Hotel—did not exist by 1871.

By 1875, reports and illustrations provide new context about Cary's built environment. One notable account describes a three-story brick building originally designed as a hotel but repurposed as a cotton mill and later as a tobacco factory.

Shortly after Cary was established in 1871, entrepreneur W.T. Blackwell considered the town as the potential site for his burgeoning tobacco business. During discussions, Blackwell questioned Frank Page about the strict enforcement of Cary's temperance stance. Page assured Blackwell that temperance would be rigorously upheld, leaving no room for exceptions for individuals or businesses. This firm stance led Blackwell to abandon his plans for Cary and instead establish his operation in Durham. By the late 1800s, the Blackwell Tobacco Company had gained immense success, naming its flagship product "Bull" Durham Tobacco. This branding earned Durham the enduring nickname "Bull City," a core identity that persists to this day.

Frank Page, however, seemed undeterred by the missed opportunity. To avoid any potential notions that his temperance principles had cost Cary's economic growth, Page may have repurposed his original hotel into a tobacco factory. While it remains unclear if the factory was ever used for tobacco production, it inadvertently became Cary's first co-working space, hosting offices, a post office, an Episcopal chapel and various local manufacturing endeavors.

Trying to create Cary's own tobacco venture landed Frank in $10,000 of debt, causing him to leave Cary for the Sandhills in search of his favorite crop: plentiful lumber. Ultimately, the factory, which was located approximately where the Cary Fire Department Administration Building is today at 100 North Academy Street, burned down and was not rebuilt. An illustration from a July 2, 1875 article depicts this building with features atypical of industrial structures: a tin-like roof, wraparound balconies and multiple doorways opening onto those balconies. These architectural elements are more consistent with a hotel design than with a factory.

The repurposing of this building suggests that Cary's early efforts to establish a grand hotel faced challenges, whether financial, logistical or influenced by shifting priorities. The building's proximity to businesses on Railroad Street (now Cedar Street) likely contributed to its transition to industrial use. Its location—approximately one hundred feet from the train depot—matches descriptions of the building that later became a tobacco factory. This structure, sometimes mistaken for the Page-Walker Hotel, was ultimately destroyed by fire in 1908, erasing a key piece of Cary's early history.

The narrative shifts definitively in 1877, with substantial evidence pointing to the construction of the Page-Walker Hotel during the second half of that year. On May 29, 1877, a newspaper report announced plans for the completion of a new hotel by July of that year. By October 23, 1877, reports confirmed the existence of a three-story brick hotel with a mansard roof—features consistent with the present-day Page-Walker Hotel. The location of this new hotel, approximately two hundred feet from the train depot, further supports its identification as the structure now known as the Page-Walker Hotel.

This timeline indicates that the Page-Walker Hotel was completed between May and October 1877. The year 1868, commonly cited as the approximate construction date, appears to be incorrect. Instead, the evidence suggests a progression of hotel development in Cary, beginning with a modest wooden structure in 1869 and culminating in the grand brick hotel known today as the Page-Walker Hotel in 1877.

Page-Walker Hotel in 1916. *Page-Walker Historical Collection.*

From this analysis, a more detailed narrative of Cary's hotel history can be constructed:

1. A Modest Wooden Hotel in 1869: The "hotel" listed in Branson's 1869 directory was likely a simple wooden building, serving as a basic lodging house for travelers and/or sawmill workers. Its absence from descriptions of Cary in 1871 suggests that it may have fallen out of use, been demolished or been repurposed by that time. This early hotel, while significant as a precursor, would have been modest compared to the grand vision Frank Page later pursued.

2. The Brick Building Turned Factory: The three-story brick building described in 1875 was initially designed as a hotel but was repurposed as a cotton mill and later a tobacco factory. Its hotel-like design, including wraparound balconies and multiple exits, hints at its original intent. The building's proximity to the train depot made it a prime candidate for industrial use, especially as Cary's economic priorities shifted. Located near the corner of Cedar and Academy Streets (the current site of the Cary Fire

Department Administration Building), this structure represents an early but ultimately unsuccessful attempt to establish a prominent hotel in Cary.

3. The Page-Walker Hotel as Cary's First Grand Hotel: Likely completed in 1877, the Page-Walker Hotel represents a significant milestone in Cary's development. Its elegant architectural style, with a mansard roof and brick construction, positioned it as a key feature of the town. Unlike its possible predecessors, this hotel endured, becoming a lasting symbol of Cary's early history.

The history of the Page-Walker Hotel reflects the complexities and challenges of small-town development in the late nineteenth century. Early mentions of a hotel in 1869 suggest modest beginnings, while the plans announced in 1871 highlight Frank Page's ambitions to create a more substantial structure. The confusion surrounding the 1875 tobacco factory underscores the fluidity of these efforts, as economic realities forced adaptations and repurposing of buildings.

Page-Walker Arts and History Center. *Carla Jordan Michaels.*

By 1877, the completion of the Page-Walker Hotel marked a turning point for Cary. This grand hotel became a focal point of the town, serving travelers and locals alike. While questions about earlier hotels and their exact locations remain, the Page-Walker Hotel stands as a testament to the vision and determination of Cary's founder.

Today, the Page-Walker Hotel, now known as the Page-Walker Arts and History Center, is the only surviving downtown structure from Cary's earliest years, solidifying its importance in Cary's history. Its preservation ensures that this chapter of Cary's history continues to be remembered and celebrated, even as the details of its origin story are reevaluated and refined through ongoing historical research.

FRANK PAGE'S CONTROVERSIAL AND MYSTERIOUS LAST YEARS

Although he tried, Frank never fully recovered financially in Cary from the Civil War, a war he correctly predicted as foolish for the South to undertake. In 1880 and $10,000 in debt, Frank bought fourteen thousand acres in Moore County and moved his family to what he perceived as greener pastures—and plentiful longleaf pine trees. He reestablished himself as a lumber man and built a sawmill business. Being a serial entrepreneur, Frank embarked in banking, a new business venture for him. Frank also built the Aberdeen and Asheboro Railroads, still prohibiting any alcohol to be carried on the rails of the tracks that he built. He continued to develop the area, much like he did for Cary. When the town of Aberdeen in Moore County was incorporated in 1889, Frank Page was credited as its founder. He is perhaps the only North Carolinian credited for founding two different North Carolina towns.

The Page family flourished in Aberdeen. Frank generated his fortune, the Page children grew into adulthood and came into their own and together Frank and Catherine rebuilt homes and their lives. On August 21, 1897, the Page family were devastated by the death of Catherine at sixty-five, a true partner to Frank and a beloved and respected mother of her children. She died suddenly and unexpectedly, after Frank reported that he left her quite healthy one morning sitting on the front porch of their home. She was surrounded by nearly all of her children when she died.

After forty-eight years of marriage to Catherine, instead of settling into a widower's life, as expected by his children, Frank began to rebel and depart from his previous self. He began to ride fast horses and behaved in other ways that shocked his adult children. He frequented Raleigh. On one of those visits, Frank was challenged by a peer that he could never build a successful "dry" hotel in Raleigh as he did in Cary. So Frank went about building the grand Park Hotel, which not only became a successful dry hotel but also became a Raleigh landmark for decades. He also built the Academy of Music on the corner of Martin and Salisbury Streets in Raleigh. Both the Park Hotel and the Academy of Music were credited in 1899 as two of the largest and most costly buildings in Raleigh.

Soon after Kate's passing and to his adult children's horror, Frank began pursuing new female companionship. In the weeks leading up to his shocking remarriage, Frank's children confronted him on what they saw as his poor judgment and disrespect to their recently passed mother through his actions. A recently discovered letter written to Frank's sister, Eliza, on October 7, 1898, by one of Frank's sons, most likely Robert Newton Page, is transcribed here in its entirety:

> *My dear Aunt Eliza,*
> *Several days ago I promised Emma* [one of Frank's other children] *that I would write to you, and the subject, of which I have wanted to write you for a month is such a distressing painful one, that I have delayed doing so from day to day—hoping that something would transpire making it unnecessary. This hope seems now vain, and we owe it to you that you should be acquainted with our trouble—for really in comparison we have never had any before, all others going away was a severe trial—but we knew she was at rest, and we "sorrowed not as those who have no hope."*
>
> *About a month ago, Pa announced one day to Ella, (Frank's* [Jr.] *wife), that he was going to be married in October.*
>
> *We had heard rumors of his paying attention to women for several months—but Aunt Eliza, I never believed one word of it. My confidence in him was unbounded—and that my father should commit such folly—before my mother had been in her grave a year, I could not believe. I know the tendency of a certain class of people to talk, and I paid very little attention to it.*
>
> *When he himself confessed it, I was shocked beyond any thing that I can express. He seemed to avoid any and all of his children, and after having told Ella—went to Myrtle with it. She blessed him out. The next day, Henry Chris, Frank, and myself sought an interview with him. I told him of the shame of it. The disgrace to him, to us, the disloyalty, and dishonor to our mother, his wife, with whom he had lived for forty-seven*

years, and who had been gone away only a year. I reminded him of his age, his physical infirmities. Every thing that could be said—we said. I told him that his death last winter when he was so very sick would have been nothing compared with the trouble he was about to bring up on us—for that would have been trouble without shame, without disgrace. We talked with him for hours—he became very angry—said we were ungrateful, that there was no disgrace, no shame in it, that we were every one fools, and that he had more sense than every child he had combined.

We made him admit that he had addressed at least two other women before this one (one of them was Mrs. Leak, a Durham widow). That he had never seen this woman, until three weeks before the time we were talking with him, and that on his second visit he addressed her, and after making all these admissions, he professed to see nothing in it that we his children had any right to object to!

I reminded him of what he said of Uncle Lewis less than a year ago, calling him an old fool and etc, and I plainly told him he was making a greater fool of himself than Uncle Lewis had or ever could. That if there ever was a combination of circumstances making it right for a man of his age to get married, there was no excuse for him, with three daughters not only devoted to him, but ready to do him any service, as in fact were all of us.

Nothing seemed to have any effect upon him, and we at last dropped the subject, and all agreed to treat him with the greatest kindness and consideration, and avoid talking about this matter at all. Things went along that way for a week and our silence led him to believe we had changed our minds about it, and he opened the question with Emma and Henry—and when they gave him to understand that not only they, but all of us stood exactly where he did, and that nothing on earth would ever make us call wrong, right—he became very violent, abused them unmercifully, ordered Henry from his house—declared that he reared a set of ungrates and fools, and declared his sorrow that he had a child in the world.

He became every day harder to approach, kept away from home for several days and when there, was shut in his room most of the time. He is far from being well and Emma and Fannie have waited on him night and day, and have not allowed his abuse to influence their action toward him in the least.

Last Tuesday night, he sent for us all, and said if he was able to get out of the bed he was going to be married the 25th of this month. Aunt Eliza, there was only one thing to tell him—and I told him as did the others that

> *he must decide between this woman that he had never seen until the last of August, and his eight children—all of whom had loved him, and would make any sacrifice that did not involve our own honor and the memory of our dead mother.*
>
> *I have at great length tried to tell you the horror in all its painful detail. He is going to marry her if God lets him live the month out, for Aunt Eliza he is insane. There is not a patient in Morganton Asylum any more so. The woman is 37 years old, a widow, and is of course marrying him for his money, the sooner he dies the better she will like it. Emma and Mary and Fannie can't live with this woman. They shall not try! This is deep water—*

On November 16, 1898, within fifteen months of becoming a widower, seventy-four-year-old Frank married Lula Brookshire McLeod, a thirty-seven-year-old widow, in Richmond County—a few weeks after Frank's stated deadline. There were married by Jesse H. Page, who was a Methodist minister and Frank's brother.

Frank and Lula lived in Raleigh, where they rented (and Lula later purchased) the Merrimon-Wynne, the former grand home of chief justice of the North Carolina Supreme Court, Augustus Summerfield Merrimon. Although moved from its original location, the Merrimon-Wynne, now in the National Register of Historic Places, still stands today and is privately owned as an event venue.

This is where hidden history becomes history's mysteries. Less than a year later, on October 16, 1899, at age seventy-five, Allison Francis Page died in the home after being unconscious for a week. One of his obituaries that appeared in newspapers across the state reported that he turned seventy-five years old just in August and that his "hale and hearty appearance then indicated that he would reach the age of his father, who died at the age of 94." There is no death certificate on record. Although this is not completely unusual before 1915, no death certificate does leave some unanswered questions, including the cause of his death.

In his last will, dated October 3, 1899, just a few days before his death, Frank's estate was valued at $60,000 (about $2.3 million in today's dollars). Frank left $5,000 to be split among his eighteen grandchildren and a generous donation to the Methodist Orphanage. His Academy of Music in Raleigh was bequeathed to the orphanage, which was to be held in trust, with half of rents and profits to be given to Lula for the length of her life and the other half to be given in support of the orphanage.

The rest of his substantial estate was also willed to Lula and her heirs. The will also states that Lula would serve as an executor of Frank's estate. She was also to determine his final resting place at Oakwood Cemetery in Raleigh, with a suitable but not costly monument erected at the site to be paid out of his estate. The three executors, which included Lula and two of Frank's lawyers, were given the power to sell any of his remaining properties at their exclusive discretion. There was no provision made in the will for his adult children, as Frank stated that he had already provided "liberally" for them previously in the conveyance of some of his property to them.

The mystery deepens regarding what happens next, but before going on, here is an introduction to the Page children. It is important to understand how high profile and achieving the Page children were not only to appreciate their individual legacies but also to truly understand the gravity of what unfolded.

The Page Children

Together, Frank and Kate had eight children, many of whom went on to achieve great things. Their children were often described as highly gifted and accomplished, and historians attribute their success to both their parents' nature and nurturing. Frank and Kate's legacy is evident in their children's significant contributions to society, which spanned various fields, including statesmanship, education, philanthropy and business.

Cary's most famous son, Walter Hines Page, was born in 1855. He went on to serve as U.S. ambassador to Great Britain under President Woodrow Wilson during World War I, where he played a key role in encouraging the United States to support the Allies. Walter was one of only three Americans honored with a plaque in Westminster Abbey. He also founded the *State Chronicle*, which would later become the *News & Observer*, and served as the editor of the *Atlantic Monthly*. Walter was instrumental in the creation of North Carolina State University and an early founder of Doubleday, which started as the publishing house Doubleday Page.

Robert Newton Page, born in 1859, became a respected legislator, congressman and banker.

Henry Allison Page Sr. (1862–1935) served as the U.S. food commissioner under President Hoover during World War I and later became president of the North Carolina Railroad.

Above: Page Aberdeen home. *704 Photography*.

Left: Page descendants in Aberdeen. *Turning the Page, Instagram.*

Emma Catherine Page (1864–1938) was a faculty member at the North Carolina College for Women for fifty years.

Junius Raboteau Page Sr. (1866–1938) became an important business leader and benefactor in Aberdeen.

Mary Esther Page (1869–1961) was known for her work as the family historian and philanthropist.

Frances Page Wilder (1872–1941) was a respected community leader in Moore County. Hers is the only remaining home of the Page children built by Frank in Aberdeen.

Frank Allison Page (1875–1934) was an engineer and businessman who founded Wachovia Bank and helped North Carolina earn the title of

"Good Roads State" through his work with the North Carolina Highway Commission.

Sadly, two of Frank and Kate's children, Sally and Raboteau, died at an early age, their causes of death unknown. Despite this heartache, Frank and Kate's family flourished, with their children contributing to a wide range of sectors and making a lasting impact on both North Carolina and the broader world.

Back to Our Story...

Frank's body was "reclaimed" by his sons. Which sons and how exactly they did it is still a bit of mystery. As for the sons who did it, remember that they were all high-profile leaders at the time. So whoever was involved, it likely would have been scandalous and risky for their careers and standing. This did not dissuade them.

As for their method, well, there are two leading theories the history trail provides. In one, Robert Newton Page (the same man who likely wrote the letter to Aunt Eliza) was one of the participants. His grandson reported that Robert and one or two of his brothers traveled to Raleigh, intending to stop Lula from burying their father in Oakwood.

They arrived at the Merrimon-Wynne house and found their father's body laid out in an upstairs room. They disapproved of the casket Lula had chosen, just as they disapproved of Lula herself. His sons felt it was a cheap, simple pine box, not at all worthy of their father. They removed their father's body from that casket and then placed it in another casket they had brought. Then they threw Lula's casket down the stairs for her to find upon returning home. When asked why Lula did not report the body snatching, Robert Page's grandson replied, "If she knew anything about my grandfather, she kept her mouth shut."

A visit to the Merrimon-Wynne today reveals that the layout of the house would have been completely conducive to this report. The original stairs land right at the entryway of the front door. Looking at the stairs, it is easy to imagine some of the larger gouges being caused by the impact of the casket as it crashed down the stairs. Imagine Lula coming back home through the front door to be greeted by Frank's destroyed and/or opened casket with his body no longer occupying it.

The second theory relies on newspaper accounts rather than family reports. Newspapers report Frank having a big funeral at Raleigh's Edenton

Graves of Frank and Catherine Page in Aberdeen. *Author's collection.*

Street Methodist Church and then being buried during a graveside service at Raleigh's Oakwood Cemetery. However, Oakwood Cemetery interment records report no Allison Francis Page (or variations of the name) buried at Oakwood.

Did Lula bury an empty casket to avoid scandal? Or did the sons recover Frank's body from the Oakwood burial site and then had his name later removed from the interment records?

We may never know if Frank's body was removed by his sons from the Merrimon-Wynne house or from the burial site in Oakwood. But we do know that Frank's final wishes were not followed for his final resting place. We also know where Frank's body ended up. His sons took his body back to Aberdeen, where it was buried at the Old Bethesda Church Cemetery, next to Catherine. His monument is more of a simple headstone made in similar fashion as Catherine's. They are surrounded by seven of their eight children.

Buried two hundred yards nearby in his own hedge-surrounded plot is the body of the remaining child, Ambassador Walter Hines Page. All remain there today, accessible to the public.

When Frank and Lula lived in the Raleigh house, it was known by its original name, Merrimon House. So how and when was the "Wynne" name added to the house? Well, to know that, the rest of the Lula B. Page story must be shared.

In 1901, Lula and the other executors of Frank's authorized the sale of the Academy of Music, then located at 304 South Salisbury Street, where the Wake County Justice Center is today, to the Auditorium Company to build an auditorium on the site. However, newspaper accounts in 1901 note that more money needed to be raised by the Auditorium Company for the auditorium's construction. J. Stanhope Wynne, secretary and treasurer of the Auditorium Company, appointed in 1901, indicated that more sources of revenue had been identified recently, ensuring its likely construction. This deal of the purchase of the Academy of Music to be repurposed for the auditorium was finalized around February 21, 1902, with Lula still owning half of the interest. The planned auditorium would be the largest in the state at the time.

On February 12, 1902, not quite two and half years after Frank's death, Lula married for the third time to J. Stanhope Wynne, treasurer of the Auditorium Company and now trustee of the Methodist Orphanage. Wynne was twelve years Lula's senior. They were married by a Presbyterian minister at the Merrimon-Wynne, where Lula had lived with Frank, where Frank died and where she continued to live afterward with Wynne. The newspaper announcement indicates that "no cards" would be sent, which generally means that the wedding was small so the couple were only personally inviting close family and friends to attend the ceremony, as opposed to mailing out invitations.

The Wynnes continued to live in the Merrimon-Wynne home for almost twenty years and raised his four children there. J. Stanhope was elected Raleigh mayor in 1909 on a reform ticket. In 1919, the Wynnes deeded the house to Peace College, after which it became known as Wynne Hall. In 1935, the mansion then served as the residence of the Peace College president for thirty years. It was listed in the National Register in 1976. In 2008, while owned by the State of North Carolina, the Merrimon-Wynne was moved from its original 526 North Wilmington Street in downtown

JANET S BYRD
903 WASHINGTON ST
CARY N C 27511 C
C 5 71

Fire Occurred
Sept. 22, 1970

Now all that is left are 200-year-old memories.

VOL. 8 NO. 39 PUBLI

NEEDED:

Cub Scoutmaster

If anyone is interest ed, please contact Pete Murdock at Pete's Hardware in Cary.

Historic Page House Goes Up In Flames

Cary News article of the Page home destruction in 1970. *Digital NC.*

Raleigh to its current location one block away at 500 North Blount Street. Due to the move, the house was then delisted from the National Register. It was reinstated at its new location in 2014. It sits there today, owned privately and operated as a special event venue.

The Wynnes eventually retired to Florida and lived their lives out together. J. Stanhope died there in 1934. Lula followed in 1944.

For his children, Frank's final years after Catherine passed remained a dark time in their lives. In fact, this second marriage was kept secret from many of Frank and Catherine's grandchildren. This led to a very uncomfortable family party in the 1930s when the grandchildren in the know brought up the subject to the other grandchildren. This surprised subgroup of grandchildren, who refused to believe it, accused the other subgroup of lying and left the party outraged.

Similarly, only one other Cary history book to date has referenced Allison Francis Page's second marriage. None of Frank's biographies mentions it. This book is the first to delve deeper into the circumstances and impact of this second marriage and beyond as a subsequent chapter in the hidden history of Cary's founder.

Cary has a few reminders of the Page family still today: the Page-Walker Hotel (home of the Page-Walker Arts and History Center), the North Carolina historical marker dedicated to Walter Hines Page, Frank's smokehouse behind the Page-Walker Hotel and the graves of several Pages at Cary's historical Hillcrest Cemetery. There are also local streets that bear their names, including Page Street off South Harrison Avenue and Ambassador Loop in front of the town hall and the Page-Walker. Unfortunately, the Page homestead burned down through somewhat controversial circumstances in 1970, just prior to Cary's planned centennial celebration in 1971.

Cary High School

The Origins of Cary High School

Cary High School is a fascinating example of history hidden in plain sight. The story of Cary High School is deeply woven into the town's origins and predates its official founding in 1871. While today's Cary High School campus sits at Walnut Street and Maynard Road, its beginnings trace back to the location now home to the Cary Arts Center, once known as the "school lot." This land has been central to Cary's educational legacy, hosting various school buildings over the years.

Before Cary's incorporation, education in the area took place either at home or in small "common schools" for those who could afford it. Frank Page, Cary's founder, had a vision for a larger, more substantial institution. Inspired by his well-educated wife, Kate, Frank made education a cornerstone of Cary's future. After surveying today's downtown to find its highest point, Frank determined that the land where the Cary Arts Center sits today would be the home of education in Cary. In 1871, he donated the four acres of oak-shaded land and materials for a schoolhouse, establishing Cary Academy, the predecessor of Cary High School.

Early Years of Cary Academy

In December 1869, Cary Academy's opening was announced, and the private boarding school officially began in January 1870. Abraham

Cary Academy students and faculty. *Page-Walker Arts and History Center/Leslie Douglas.*

Haywood Merritt, a University of North Carolina graduate, became the first principal. Merritt was a well-respected local figure and Methodist church member, and he quickly built the school's reputation. Cary Academy attracted students from across the state, with families sending their children to board and attend the school. Several other private schools opened nearby, but Cary Academy expanded beyond the traditional one-room model and left a lasting legacy.

The school's first building—a two-story, four-room structure—was completed in early 1871 to accommodate a growing student body. However, lingering economic challenges from the Civil War led Frank Page to sell one-third of his interest in the school to Rufus Jones in 1873 as Frank moved with his family to Moore County to rebuild his fortune. By 1873, Page had sold his remaining interest in the school to two of Jones's daughters, and the Jones family, all teachers, became closely involved with Cary Academy. During this period, Frank's brother, Reverend Jesse Page, served as principal from 1873 to 1877, maintaining the Page family values at the school.

Cary Academy was committed to high academic standards and discipline, but its mission adapted to the community's evolving needs. The school sometimes operated as a coeducational institution, a girls' school or a teacher training institute, reflecting the changing educational landscape.

The school had several principals in its early years, including the notable Reverend Solomon Pool, a former president of the University of North Carolina at Chapel Hill. Pool became principal of Cary Academy in the early 1880s after a controversial end to his tenure at UNC. Pool became president at UNC in 1869 amid the university's struggles to recover from the devastation of the Civil War. The campus buildings were in disrepair, and enrollment had dwindled, which led Pool to propose a radical solution.

Cary Academy, 1870s. *Page-Walker Historical Collection.*

He controversially stated that if white students did not return, he would open enrollment to African American students. This position, alongside his criticism of the university's governance, which he believed was too heavily influenced by the elite interests of eastern North Carolina, made him a target of criticism. Pool's call for "loyalizing" the institution, preferring it closed over continuing as a "nursery of treason," further alienated many, ultimately leading to his ouster in 1875 by court order.

After his removal from UNC, Pool's career took a different path when he accepted the position of principal at Cary Academy in 1871. Frank Page offered Pool the use of a house, today known as the Sams Jones House, owned today by the Town of Cary and located at the corner of Academy Street and Dry Avenue. Although the house suffered fire and rebuilding, it remains a contributing property to Cary's designated Downtown Historic District. For three years, Pool led the institution during its formative years, a critical time of reconstruction following the Civil War and just after Cary's founding.

TRANSITION TO CARY HIGH SCHOOL

A new chapter for the school began in 1896 when it was formally incorporated as Cary High School, thanks to the leadership of Principal E.L. Middleton and the support of local stockholders C.W. Blanchard, F.R. Gray, C.W. Scott, A.D. Hunter, J.C. Angier and J.E. White. Middleton, with a solid educational background and experience at the Wilson Male Academy and the Durham Female Institute, brought stability and vision to the growing institution. His efforts, along with the support of the new board, led to the school's official incorporation by the State of North Carolina on July 24, 1896, as Cary High School, following its purchase from the Jones family.

In the school's incorporation announcement, Cary is described as "both healthful and beautiful. The moral atmosphere of the town of Cary could be not excelled in the State. The society in the town…[is] elevating and stimulating….No better railroad facility could be furnished in the State—just at the junction of the Seaboard and Southern Railways. It is far removed from the malarial regions, with pure, cold well-water in abundance as the beverage of the people. The town was chartered dry, and is fortified against the possibility of alcoholic drinks ever being sold in or near it."

Middleton's commitment to high standards in education quickly raised the school's profile, attracting more students and necessitating expansions.

Additional classroom wings and dormitories were added to accommodate both local students and those coming from farther away, as Cary High School became known for offering a superior education. While not affiliated with any particular religious denomination, the school encouraged a "broad and liberal Christian spirit," focusing on both intellectual and moral development. As of 1900, census reports the population of the village of Cary had grown to 333 people.

Principal Middleton regularly advertised and marketed the school to further increase enrollment. But he was very specific on the ideal students he was seeking for the school. Boy students should be "of good habits who want an education and willing to work for it." They should not "curse, swear, play cards, and use intoxicants." Girl students are those "who prefer well-stored brains and countenances beaming with intelligence to servile obedience to the whims of fashion." They should not be "unwilling to obey rules made for their welfare and protection." Middleton also made it clear that Cary High School was not a reformatory school, stating, "However much we may be interested in the reformation of bad boys, we could not take the risk of endangering the character of many others for the hope of benefitting one." Keep in mind, Cary High School at this time was still a private boarding school. As of 1905, student enrollment was 182, with

Cary High School playground, 1910s. *Page-Walker Arts and History Center/Leslie Douglas.*

Cary High School cornerstone. *Author's collection.*

109 boarders and 73 local students. It had been historically the largest boarding school in Wake County.

In March 1907, the North Carolina General Assembly voted to establish a statewide system of public high school, promising to match local funding dollar for dollar, provided these schools operated at least five months a year and paid teachers a minimum of $40 per month. Immediately upon this action, stockholders urged the Wake County Board of Education to buy Cary High School for $2,750 to become a publicly funded school under this new legislation. Just eight days after the enabling legislation passes, the Board of Education agreed to the purchase, being the first to trigger this newly offered state support. This made Cary High School the first publicly funded high school in the North Carolina, with half of the purchase price coming from the state.

Hence Cary High School, founded in 1870 as a private school called Cary Academy, became North Carolina's first public high school on April 6, 1907, under this new initiative. The state then created the Cary School District and authorized citizens living in the defined district to vote on a local school tax of up to 30 cents per $100 personal property valuation. The tax was approved by Cary residents by a margin of 100 to 2 on May 7, 1907. This further allowed for Cary High School to continue to meet its public support test required by the new legislation.

Middleton's tenure lasted until 1908, when he left to become the first Sunday school secretary of the North Carolina Baptist State Convention, a position that allowed him to focus on his passion for establishing Sunday schools. His departure marked the end of an era for Cary High School but left a foundation of strong academics and values that the school would continue to build on.

THE LEGACY OF MARCUS BAXTER DRY

In 1908, thirty-seven-year-old Marcus Baxter Dry, an increasingly prominent educator in North Carolina, took over as principal, continuing to uphold and further develop the school's commitment to high-quality education. He lived at 400 Faculty Avenue at the intersection with Dry Avenue, within earshot of the school. The house still stands today and is known as the Marcus Dry House. Dry Avenue, which passes right along the side of his house, is named for Marcus Dry, Cary High School's longest-standing principal, not because Cary was founded as a "dry" town.

Under Dry's leadership, the school remained an important community hub, hosting regular social events like picnics and barbecues at the start of each school term. The school's assembly halls also served as venues for speeches and performances by prominent visitors to Cary, reinforcing its role as a central gathering place.

In 1913, a new brick building was constructed, the first of six major additions that turned the school into an architectural model for others. Dry also heralded an age of innovation for the school. He advocated for

Principal Marcus Dry's house. *Author's collection.*

a flexible approach to education, focusing on both rigorous academic preparation for college-bound students and practical vocational training for those aiming to work within their communities. He introduced agricultural and home economics classes through a newly founded Farm-Life Department. Dry also pioneered vocational training for children with developmental disabilities. Through his "Betterment Association," a precursor to the Parent-Teacher Association, Dry introduced hot lunch programs, and he launched other initiatives. Records from the 1920s indicate that Cary High School attracted students from distant regions, including Virginia and South Carolina.

Dry continued to innovate at Cary High, introducing a student council in 1919, a public school music program and band in 1922 and a commercial department in 1924. In 1925, Cary High added the first gymnasium at a rural high school in the state, and between 1922 and 1928, it hosted a teacher training program backed by the North Carolina Department of Education. Cary High's proximity to Raleigh and Dry's progressive initiatives made it a model institution within North Carolina's public school system. Principals from other schools often sought Dry's guidance on effective school leadership.

The economic hardship of the 1929 stock market crash and the subsequent Depression brought new challenges. Yearbooks were discontinued until after World War II, leaving few detailed records of student life during this period. Although school newspapers attempted to fill the gap, few survived, limiting insight into this era. However, the school remained a focal point for the community.

Transportation advances, particularly the introduction of school buses, also altered Cary High School's character. Buses enabled students who would have boarded at Cary to attend new regional schools closer to their homes, leading the high school to become primarily local. By 1933, Cary's dormitories had closed, and the former girls' dormitory, the Frank Page Dormitory, was converted into a "Teacherage," offering apartments for married teachers and rooms for single teachers.

In 1939, the original 1913 school building was replaced with a new structure, marking the dedication of the building specifically for Dry, the first North Carolina principal recognized for "wearing out" a schoolhouse through decades of dedicated service. The 1939 graduation ceremony had to be held at various locations around town due to construction. A memorable moment from that year's commencement was the speech by gubernatorial candidate J.M. Broughton at the First Baptist Church

Cary High School farm life barn, 1920. *Page-Walker Arts and History Center/Leslie Douglas.*

Cary High School. *Page-Walker Arts and History Center/Leslie Douglas.*

Cary High School, 1941. *Page-Walker Arts and History Center/Leslie Douglas.*

in downtown. Unaware of the church's rule against applause, he was initially disheartened by the silence following his speech, only to learn that absolute decorum was expected in the sanctuary—a discovery that reportedly led him to avoid future speeches at Baptist churches.

In 1942, an era ended as Dry stepped down as principal of Cary High School, concluding thirty-four years of service in Cary and a remarkable fifty-one years in education. His contributions to education in Cary were transformative, with his innovative approach to both academic and vocational training admired and emulated throughout North Carolina. Standing over six feet tall with dark hair and eyes, Dry was known for his formal manner yet genial spirit. His students admired his dedication, and many went on to achieve significant success in education, business and other professional fields. Dry was also an active member of the Cary Baptist Church, where he taught the Men's Bible Class for more than thirty years, which was named in his honor. In 1930, in recognition of his influence, his students and congregation sent him on a trip to the Holy Land, including visits to thirteen European countries.

During World War II, Cary High School continued to operate, but by 1944, enrollment had dropped to its lowest level in about thirty years. Following the war's end, life slowly returned to normal both in the community and at the school. Within a decade, enrollment nearly doubled. The yearbook resumed publication in 1945, and in 1948, it was renamed *YRAC*, Cary spelled backward, a name that has endured.

Married to Wilma Annie Perry, Dry had three children: Helen, William and Hallie. Following his death in 1946, a bronze plaque and portrait honoring Dry was placed in the school building. He is buried at Cary's historic Hillcrest Cemetery, near the school he served for so long, leaving a legacy of dedication, progress and community impact.

Belvin Maynard Flyover of Cary High School

Belvin Maynard, known as the "Flying Parson," was a significant figure in early aviation history, particularly noted for his achievements during and after World War I. Born in 1894 in Anson County, North Carolina, Maynard initially pursued a path in ministry but found his calling in aviation when he enlisted in the U.S. Army during the war. Trained as a pilot, he quickly became the chief test pilot for new aircraft at an airfield in France, where his skills garnered attention, including a world record for executing 318 consecutive loops in a single flight.

After the war, Maynard's exploits continued to capture the public's imagination. He participated in high-profile air races, gaining fame as the "greatest pilot on earth." His notable victory in the 1919 air race from Long Island to San Francisco, where he completed the journey in just fifty hours despite numerous challenges, solidified his reputation. Maynard combined his passions for aviation and ministry, often preaching and conducting weddings mid-flight, further endearing him to the public.

In 1920, after establishing himself as a celebrated pilot, Lieutenant Belvin Maynard visited Cary High School, then located at the end of Academy Street in downtown Cary. This marked his first stop after returning from World War I, inspired by the invitation of a former classmate who was then a teacher at the school. He brought along his beloved German shepherd, Trixie, who was frequently seen by his side in the plane.

The day after his visit, Maynard fulfilled his promise to say goodbye on his way out of town by conducting a thrilling "*Top Gun*–like" flyover that captivated students and residents alike. As his plane approached the school, the excitement was palpable, and the students rushed outside to witness the spectacle. Local newspaper accounts reported that he flew so low that the children could see and hear him greeting them, while Trixie barked excitedly from the passenger seat as they soared by.

Tragically, Maynard's promising career was cut short when he died in a plane crash during a stunt performance in Vermont in 1922. His untimely death brought an end to a remarkable chapter in aviation history, but his legacy as a pioneering pilot and inspirational figure continues to be celebrated in North Carolina and beyond. So, the next time you find yourself stopped at the red light facing the Cary Arts Center, which once housed Cary High School, take a moment to imagine the excitement of that day when Maynard's flyover delighted everyone in Cary.

It's worth noting that Cary's Maynard Avenue is not named after Lieutenant Maynard; rather, it derives its name from Maynard Farm, which occupied the land where the street is today. This same Maynard family also donated the land for the current location of Cary High School, providing further context for the street's name.

LIVES OF SERVICE IN EDUCATING CARY

Many teachers were instrumental in shaping the school and its students. One such notable, Miss Irma Ellis, was the granddaughter of Henry B. Jordan, a founding member of the Cary Town Council and former mayor of Cary. "Miss Irma" was known as a strict but beloved teacher who never married but instead dedicated her life to educating the future of Cary. Miss Ellis was known as an innovator in the classroom. At the time, there was no formal system for grouping students by ability or achievement, so she took the initiative to create one. However, she was mindful of the potential stigma and unhealthy competition that could arise if students knew their own or one another's rankings. To avoid this, she chose not to use traditional labels like Group A, B or C or numbers like 1, 2 or 3. Instead, she named the groups after animals or mythical creatures, which suggested no hierarchy. Versions of this approach are still used in classrooms today. Miss Ellis retired in 1950 at the age of seventy. Miss Irma taught generations of Cary children to read and other first-grade milestones, including many of Cary's future elected and community leaders.

Another influential educator was Rufus Sheldon "Dad" Dunham. A graduate of North Carolina State University in 1930, Dunham dedicated forty years to teaching agriculture at Cary High. He maintained a consistent presence over the years, earning him the affectionate nickname "Dad." Not only was he a respected teacher at the school, but he was also an admired Sunday school teacher at First Baptist Church, known for his dry wit. His wife, Rachel, had been a boarding student at Cary and married "Dad" after returning from teacher training. In his honor, Dad Dunham Park on Walnut Street bears his name.

Cary High School has long been celebrated for its outstanding music program, with piano and violin instruction part of the curriculum from its earliest days. A marching band was introduced in 1922, and by 1923, school committee minutes reveal that band members were granted "the privilege of selling refreshments at commencement" to fundraise for equipment.

The Cary High School Marching Band achieved local, national and international recognition under the direction of band directors Harold Burt, Jack White and Jimmy Burns. Harold Burt, initially hired as an industrial arts teacher, began the band program part time and taught at Cary for five years before expanding his success to other schools across Wake and Johnston Counties. Fondly remembered as Cary's "Music Man," he laid the foundation for the band's future achievements.

Cary High School majorettes, part of the band. *Page-Walker Arts and History Center/Leslie Douglas.*

Jack White, a talented jazz trumpeter and charismatic leader, later became band director at Elon College. Known for his community contributions, White also began the long-standing Cary Band Day tradition in the late 1950s.

Jimmy Burns took the Cary High School Marching Band to new heights, leading them to performances at prestigious events like the Rose Bowl Parade and international venues, including a memorable trip to Switzerland. Under his direction, the band gained national and international recognition. Burns placed great emphasis on the band's appearance, often walking around male band members before public performances, using scissors to trim any hair that touched the collar of their uniforms. He frequently reminded the band that they were representing Cary on global stages.

Over two decades of intense use and continued school growth had taken a toll on Cary High School's third building. Plans for a new high school were set in motion, and in May 1960, the third building hosted its final high school graduation. Afterward, the building was repurposed to serve as Cary Elementary, Junior High School and eventually the Cary Arts Center.

First Desegregated High School in Wake County

The new Cary High School was constructed on Walnut Street, on land previously owned by Luther Maynard, a farmer and sawmill owner. His family is also the namesake of Maynard Road. Maynard had even provided wood for the football field light poles at the previous school site.

It was at this new Walnut Street campus that Cary High School became the first desegregated high school in the county in the 1960s. Arch Arrington, a prominent member of the African American community, and Henry Adams, pharmacist who owned Adams Drug Store (the predecessor to Ashworth's Drug Store), worked together in the desegregation of Cary's schools.

On August 30, 1963, six young African American women integrated Cary High School: Brenda Hill, Esther Mayo, Phyllis McIver, Francis White, Gwen Matthews and Lucille Evans. It was theorized that the all-female class might be better received than males. Decades later, Ms. Matthews still remembers stepping off the school bus to a group yelling at her, "Two, four, six, eight, we don't want to integrate!" She did not want to return the following day, but her parents reassured her that it would get better. The demonstration group numbered around fifty, which Ms. Matthews later reasoned was not many for the size of Cary High School. Each day, Ms. Matthews reported that the protesting group was smaller and had stopped altogether by the tenth day. Wake County closely monitored Cary's progress and was delighted when no organized community opposition developed and was particularly impressed with Principal Paul Cooper's leadership and reputation for "running a tight ship" and refusing to "tolerate any foolishness" at his school. These heroes allowed for Cary to lead the way for Cary and Wake County's desegregation and for the rest of North Carolina to follow suit.

The site where Cary High School first stood at the end of South Academy has evolved into a key part of Cary's historical and cultural heritage. The Cary Arts Center, now housed in this historic property, serves as a vibrant hub for learning, performing arts and community engagement. It also stands in commemoration of Frank Page's initial educational vision, continued by world-class faculty and leaders that greatly influenced the establishment of public education in North Carolina.

Cary's Favorite Sons

Although Cary is home to many legacy families whose contributions continue to shape the town, the remarkable achievements of two men, who rose to international prominence through their distinguished diplomatic service, remain less known, possibly due to the passage of time and the overshadowing influence of more widely recognized historical figures.

Alfred Daniel "Buck" Jones

Frank Page is not the only Cary leader who met an unexpected end. Cary's favorite son, Alfred Daniel "Buck" Jones, also faced an unsettling and mysterious conclusion to his life.

Buck Jones, a prominent figure both locally and internationally, experienced a notable yet tragic life. His ancestry is deeply rooted in North Carolina history, as he was a descendant of Nathaniel Jones of White Plains. Born on July 3, 1857, in Cary, Buck pursued education rigorously, culminating in his graduation from the University of North Carolina at Chapel Hill in 1877. His impressive commencement address, "The Teacher Must Be Taught," on the importance of normal institutes, received spontaneous applause several times during the speech.

Jones began his career in law, passing the bar in 1881, and he subsequently practiced in Raleigh. His first case, in January 1877, was for Caryite C.C. Jewell, charged with selling liquor without a license. Demonstrating legal skill and persuasion, Jones secured a not guilty verdict for Jewell, especially impressive considering Cary's stout devotion to and incorporation mandated temperance.

In November 1880, Jones ran as a Democrat for the North Carolina House of Representatives, serving from January 7, 1891, to January 3, 1893. He was elected Wake County treasurer in November 1884 and became a founding member of the original Watauga Club in May 1894. This club of young professionals focused on North Carolina's future, successfully advocating for the establishment of what is now North Carolina State University. Among its notable members was Walter Hines Page, eldest child of Frank and Catherine Page, who would later become U.S. ambassador to Great Britain.

Buck's oratory skills and dedication to public service earned him a significant appointment as U.S. consul general in Shanghai by President Grover Cleveland in May 1893. However, his tenure was brief and marked by tragedy. Shortly after his arrival in Shanghai in August 1893, Jones fell seriously ill. Although it was initially thought to be malaria, his condition worsened rapidly. Reports of mental instability surfaced, allegedly linked to a romantic disappointment in North Carolina.

His deteriorating mental state led to his removal from his post and his boarding of the *Saikyō Maru* to return to the United States. During the journey, he was transferred to the steamer SS *City of Rio de Janeiro*. Tragically, his condition worsened, requiring restraints by the ship's crew. Reports varied widely, with some alleging violent outbursts and others describing a frail and comatose man with additional rumors spreading about a cursed ship.

On December 9, 1893, at age forty-eight, Buck passed away before reaching home. His body, initially embalmed aboard the ship, was re-embalmed in San Francisco amid conflicting reports about his condition. Some officials worked to control the narrative, refuting claims of violence and insanity.

Buck's body was transported by special train to Cary, accompanied by a delegation from Raleigh, including Frank Page. His devastated mother, Mary E. Jones Whitaker, greeted his casket, remarking that it was her practice to meet her son halfway upon his return home, and would do so again for his final journey.

His funeral at White Plains Methodist Episcopal Church drew thousands, including dignitaries, state officials and everyday people, African American and white, openly mourning. He was buried with full Masonic honors at Hillcrest Cemetery in Cary.

Beyond his diplomatic service, Buck left a lasting local legacy by donating land and a log cabin for Cary's first public school for African American children. This act of generosity profoundly affected the local community, providing access to education for children who had long been underserved. By prioritizing educational opportunities for African American students, Buck laid a foundation for future advancements in equality and civic development in Cary, cementing his legacy as a visionary advocate for progress. Today, his name lives on through Buck Jones Road, ensuring that his story remains a part of Cary's history.

Walter Hines Page

Walter Hines Page, born on August 15, 1855, in Cary, North Carolina, was a prominent journalist, publisher and diplomat. He is perhaps Cary's most famous son, yet his impactful contributions remain largely unknown beyond a highway marker on Chatham Street and a likely unrealized reference in the Ambassador Loop street name.

Walter, nicknamed "Wat" by his family, was the first of Frank and Catherine Page's eight children. This family connection to Cary deeply influenced his life and career.

Walter's education included the Bingham School, Trinity College (now Duke University) and Randolph-Macon College, from which he graduated in 1875. He pursued graduate studies at Johns Hopkins University and briefly taught at the University of North Carolina. His passion for journalism soon took precedence, leading him to Missouri and then New York, where he worked for the *New York World*.

Walter Hines Page. *Wikimedia Commons.*

In 1883, Walter returned to North Carolina to establish the *State Chronicle*, a weekly newspaper in Raleigh that later became the *News & Observer* in 1892. Financially backed by his father, Frank Page, Walter's newspaper emphasized substance over sensationalism. During this time, he cofounded the Watauga Club, advocating for the state's economic and social betterment. The club's efforts were instrumental in establishing North Carolina State University.

Walter's commitment to education reform extended to the Southern Education Board and the General Education Board, where he directed campaigns and distributed funds to improve education across the South. His 1896 speech, "The Rebuilding of Old Commonwealths," delivered in Greensboro, launched a public school campaign with a lasting impact on the region.

Walter's career shifted nationally in 1885 when he moved to New York, becoming editor of the *Atlantic Monthly* and cofounding Doubleday, Page & Company, a prominent publishing firm. He also founded *World's Work*, a monthly magazine pioneering the use of photographs alongside articles.

Walter's support for Woodrow Wilson's 1912 presidential campaign marked his transition to diplomacy. Appointed U.S. ambassador to Great Britain in 1913, he played a crucial role in fostering Anglo-American relations during World War I. As he was a staunch advocate for the Allied cause, Walter's efforts sometimes clashed with Wilson's initial neutrality stance. Despite challenges, his contributions were significant, earning him

Memorial plaque to Ambassador Walter Hines Page in Westminster Abbey. *Caroline McWilliams, Walter Hines Page Chapter of the National Society of the Daughters of the American Revolution (UK).*

posthumous recognition of a plaque in Westminster Abbey. The inscription honors him as the "Friend of Britain in Her Sorest Need," acknowledging his critical role in fostering close Anglo-American relations during the war. Walter is one of only three Americans to be memorialized in Westminster Abbey, a testament to his significant contributions to international diplomacy. He is also credited with creating the idea of the president's State of the Union address for President Wilson, a hallmark of every presidency that continues to this day.

Health issues forced Walter to resign in 1918. He returned to North Carolina, where he passed away on December 21, 1918, in Pinehurst. He is buried near the Page family plot at Old Bethesda Cemetery in Aberdeen, his grave adorned with American flags and tributes to his service.

Walter Hines Page's life was marked by a dedication to progress and reform. His work in education, journalism and diplomacy left an enduring legacy, ensuring that his contributions are remembered both locally and internationally. Despite his enormous achievements, his story remains a quieter chapter of Cary's history. However, the only North Carolina historical marker in Cary belongs to Water Hines Page. It is located at 149 East Chatham Street in downtown Cary—just four hundred yards from where he was born at the former Page homestead, now Cary Town Hall.

Through the lives of Alfred Daniel "Buck" Jones and Walter Hines Page, Cary's historical tapestry is enriched with stories of ambition, dedication and far-reaching impact. These two remarkable individuals, with deep roots in Cary, rose to prominence on national and international stages, leaving legacies that extend well beyond the borders of their hometown.

Hidden History Spots

Hillcrest Cemetery

At the top of a hill, Page Road dead-ends at Hillcrest Cemetery, Cary's historic cemetery. It's an easy walk from downtown, and with the new Higgins Greenway soon connecting directly to the cemetery, its status as one of Cary's hidden history spots may soon be a thing of the past. It spans 4.9 acres just south of downtown and is surrounded by wooded residential neighborhoods on all sides. Most of the cemetery was acquired by the town through multiple transactions in the 1960s and 1970s. It holds more than 2,400 burial plots and remains an active cemetery. In 2014, it was designated as a Cary historic landmark.

Though now owned by the Town of Cary, Hillcrest Cemetery has a rich history. Originally, the property was owned by R.O. Heater, known as "Mr. Cary" for his well-known enthusiasm for all things Cary. He transferred the first parcels, known as the "old section," to the Hillcrest Cemetery Association on June 11, 1945. George Turner added more land to the cemetery ten years later, and by 1970, these sections were transferred to the Town of Cary, with additional parcels added in 1977.

The earliest recorded birthdate grave belongs to Henry Jones, born on January 29, 1766. Jones, the son of Nathaniel Jones of Crabtree and husband to Nancy Jones, lived in a historic home built in 1803 on Chapel Hill Road, now known as the Nancy Jones House, a historic landmark. The earliest recorded death is that of Nathaniel Jones, who passed away on August 31,

1840, just forty days before Henry Jones. Interestingly, this Nathaniel Jones does not belong to either the White Plains or Crabtree families. There are at least ten gravestones that are unreadable or unmarked, leaving their identities a mystery, perhaps predating the Jones burials.

The "skyline" of Hillcrest Cemetery showcases an intriguing variety of grave markers, from traditional headstones to more unique designs like box tombs and obelisks. The cemetery is also home to numerous artistic engravings, symbols, statues and benches.

The monument for C.M. Baucom features the emblem of the Order of Railway Conductors, Scottish Rite. The lantern on the monument, resembling a grenade, is easily recognizable, but the other tool depicted remains unidentified. Baucom was a Seaboard freight conductor and served in the Spanish-American War and World War I.

Religious symbols are prominent throughout Hillcrest, with images such as praying hands, crowns symbolizing victory and divine sovereignty and crosses in various forms. The cemetery also features symbols from secret societies, clubs and fraternal organizations, with Masonic symbols being the most common. More than a dozen markers bear the square and compass, symbols of Freemasonry, a society well-known for its mysteries.

Touring Hillcrest is like walking through Cary's history. The cemetery is the final resting place for many notable and everyday Cary citizens, including the following.

CAPTAIN HARRISON P. GUESS (1827–1919): Among Cary's first railroad men, Guess's name is still familiar today, associated with the historic Guess-Ogle "Pink House" in downtown Cary.

DR. J.M. TEMPLETON (1855–1932): One of Cary's earliest doctors, Templeton was a crusader for prohibition, public education and economic justice. His gravestone carries the inscription, "A country doctor who served his nation in the time of war, his community in the time of peace, the rich and poor alike."

MARCUS BAXTER DRY (1871–1946): Dry served as principal of Cary High School for thirty-four years, and his influence and leadership in education are apparent not only in Cary history but also across North Carolina, as Cary High School emerged as the first public high school in North Carolina under his leadership. Dry Avenue is named in his honor.

DR. FRANK YARBOROUGH (1895–1957): Yarborough was another early physician in Cary, and his home is still on Academy Street. A portion of it facing East Park Street served as his practice. Being Cary's physician during segregation, Dr. Yarborough was forced to have two separate doors for

African American and white patients. However, showing his disdain for the requirement, he designed both doors to feed into the same waiting room.

Tragically, Dr. Yarborough's daughter, Mary Ray, who is also buried in the family plot, died at eleven from meningitis. Dr. Yarborough carried profound guilt his whole life for not being able to save his own child, who was the apple of his eye. The family plot is adorned with a bust statue of the little girl, who affectionately called Dr. Yarborough "Daddy Blue-Eyes."

ALFRED DANIEL "BUCK" JONES (1857–1893): Grandson of Nathaniel Jones of White Plains, one of Cary's early founders and a Revolutionary War Patriot, Buck had a deep connection to Cary. He donated his own land and log cabin to establish one of the first public schools for African American children in Cary. In 1891, he was elected to the North Carolina House of Representatives, and in 1893, he was appointed by President Grover Cleveland as consul general of the United States to Shanghai. He contracted malaria there and died on the ship returning to Cary under somewhat mysterious circumstances, discussed in more detail previously. His funeral in 1893 drew thousands of mourners, a number far exceeding Cary's population at the time. When his casket arrived, his mother rushed out to meet it, as was their habit to meet her son halfway upon arriving home.

FRED GAINES BOND (1929–1997): Bond served as Cary mayor from 1971 to 1983, and his name may be recognizable given the popular Cary park that bears his name. When Bond joined the Cary Town Council in 1965, the town's population was just seven thousand. He was committed to preserving Cary's small-town character even as it expanded. During his time in office, Bond established an appearance commission, launched a downtown improvement program and oversaw the construction of a new town hall and library. In a 1997 obituary, Mayor Koka Booth remarked, "Whatever Cary was and whatever Cary will be, was because of Fred Bond's leadership." Mayor Bond is the uncle of current Cary Mayor Harold Weinbrecht.

JOSEPH CEPHUS MATTHEWS SR. (1857–1937): J.C. Matthews was a skilled carpenter and lumberman who ran his own sawmill in Cary. With his expertise, he constructed a grand Greek Revival home for his family using high-quality lumber from his mill. This house, still known today as the Matthews House, located at 317 West Chatham Street, became a prominent and one of the largest residences in Cary at the time. It has been owned by many well-known Cary residents and is currently a special event venue and bar.

REBEKAH LEE MATTHEWS (1954–1970): On December 23, Rebekah was killed tragically in a hit-and-run accident just one hundred yards from making it back home on Kildaire Farm Road after Christmas shopping. The perpetrator was never charged. Rebekah was part of the Matthews family, responsible for building the Matthews House. She is not buried with other members of the Matthews family at Hillcrest given that the family did not have plot ready for her due to her young age. The Cary town manager at the time donated his plot at Hillcrest for her burial.

Henry Adams (1899–1968): Henry Adams owned two businesses at the corner of Chatham and Academy Streets: Adams Drug Store, later Ashworth's Drugs, and Adams Appliance Store. In addition to being a businessman, he served on the school board and led efforts to integrate Cary's schools, allowing for Cary High School to become the first integrated school in Wake County. Adams Elementary School was named in his honor.

Dorothy Mae Neville (1933–1950): Dorothy, a student at Cary High School, tragically lost her life in a freak accident while having lunch with friends near the school's flagpole when the school was located in downtown Cary. The flag halyard snapped, causing the flag and its cable to be carried by the wind about fifteen to twenty feet before hitting a twelve-thousand-volt power line. Due to frayed insulation from age and weather, the line sparked, igniting the flag and causing the cable to strike Dorothy, leading to her electrocution. Her family later filed a lawsuit against the power company, which resulted in statewide improvements in the management and maintenance of power lines.

Russell O. Heater (1895–1971): Known as a prominent early developer in Cary, Russell Heater was responsible for creating neighborhoods like Sunset Hills, Veteran Hills and Russell Hills. Veteran Hills was developed by Mr. Heater specifically for veterans returning from war. Many of the streets there are named for the original veterans who had houses in the development. Often referred to as "Mr. Cary" because of his tireless cheerleading and advocacy of all things Cary, Mr. Heater also served on both the Cary Town Council and the Wake County Commission. In addition to his civic work, he was deeply involved in the Methodist Church, Boy Scouts and the Masonic Lodge. He personally took care of the Hillcrest Cemetery grounds for twenty-five years.

James L. Templeton (1855–1932): One of Cary's earliest doctors, Dr. Templeton traveled by horse and buggy to make house calls for $1.50. He tended patients regardless of their ability to pay. He served as Cary's mayor from 1912 to 1916, advocating for causes such as prohibition, fair treatment of farmers, public education and improved roads. At sixty-two, when the United States entered World War I, he enlisted in the army as a physician. When he returned home, he often continued to wear his uniform, so proud

Flagpole in front of Cary Arts Center, former site of Cary Academy and Cary High School. *Author's collection.*

he was of his service. Upon returning for the war, he allowed that one shot of liquor could be used to medicinal purposes.

RUFUS HENRY JONES (1819–1903): A key figure in Cary's early history, Rufus Jones was an educator by profession. He also served as a county commissioner and represented his community in the North Carolina General Assembly. In 1857, he helped establish the Cary Masonic Lodge. Together with his daughters, Sarah and Loulie, Jones acquired Cary Academy, which later became Cary High School, North Carolina's first publicly funded school. He donated land for the creation of Hillcrest Cemetery.

HENRY B. JORDAN (1834–1914): As one of the first town commissioners when Cary was founded by Frank Page, Henry Jordan played a key role in the town's early leadership. Jordan also served as Cary's mayor from 1904 to 1910. He was also a farmer, shopkeeper and railroad station agent.

RACHEL EATON DUNHAM (1904–2001) Rachel Dunham was a Cary Highh School teacher and was instrumental in starting Cary's Gourd Village Garden Club, which led to Cary becoming the Gourd Capital of the World, as identified in the town seal for many years. She was married to and buried alongside Sheldon "Dad" Dunham Sr., who taught agriculture for forty years at Cary High School.

Hillcrest Cemetery is more than just a peaceful final resting place. It is a hidden chronicle of Cary's history, often overlooked by those who don't seek it out. Through ongoing preservation efforts, the creation of a self-guided walking tour by the Friends of the Page-Walker and the new Higgins Greenway providing easier access, this historic site is poised to become a prominent destination for those looking to explore Cary's rich past.

BARNABUS JONES FARM

The legacy of Captain Etheldred Jones and his descendants stands as a testament to the endurance of a family and their deep connection to the land. Captain Etheldred Jones, born in 1749, played a crucial role in the early history of Wake County, North Carolina, and his impact reverberated through generations, shaping the agricultural, social and cultural landscape of the region. His legacy endures today, particularly through the land he and his descendants farmed for more than two centuries. This hidden history remains a significant, though often seldom seen, part of Cary's narrative.

Etheldred Jones's life began against the backdrop of a nation on the brink of revolution. Born in 1749 in North Carolina, he became a soldier in the Continental army during the Revolutionary War. As part of General Nathanael Greene's forces, Jones participated in several pivotal battles, including the Battle of Cowpens in 1781 and the Battle of Guilford Courthouse in 1781. These battles were crucial in the fight for American independence, and Jones's service in these engagements earned him a place in the annals of local history. His preferred sidearm, a long sword, is still on display at the Guilford Courthouse National Military Park museum.

After the war, Jones settled in the Swift Creek area of Wake County, a portion of which is located in today's Cary, North Carolina. In 1790, he was granted land by the state that was located in a fertile region along Penny Road. This land would become the foundation of the Jones family homestead, a place that would serve not only as a home for Jones and his descendants but also as a site of agricultural prosperity. Etheldred Jones established a farm that became an integral part of the local economy. His home was described as a welcoming place, often hosting travelers and serving as a sanctuary for those in need. His generosity and connections to the community further cemented his importance in the region.

When he passed away in 1835, the Jones family continued to steward the land he had established, keeping alive the traditions of hard work and hospitality that he had championed. In 1859, the legacy of Captain Etheldred Jones was passed to his grandson, Barnabus Jones. Barnabus inherited 313 acres along what is now Penny Road, continuing the family's agricultural legacy in the Swift Creek region. As a farmer, Barnabus worked the land with the same dedication his grandfather had shown. The farm under his stewardship was typical of mid-nineteenth-century North Carolina agricultural practices, with a combination of crop fields, pastures and an orchard. The fertile soil of the area allowed for the cultivation of a variety of crops, including fruits and vegetables, while livestock—such as cows and poultry—ensured the farm's sustainability.

Barnabus Jones's farm became a cornerstone of the local rural economy. His dedication to his land was matched by his commitment to the community. However, the land's historical significance was marked by more than just its agricultural success. During the Civil War, the Jones farm found itself caught in the path of General William Tecumseh Sherman's infamous march through North Carolina. Sherman's troops passed through the area in 1865, and as was typical of such marches, the soldiers seized provisions and resources from local farms.

When Sherman's men arrived at the Jones farm, they took nearly all the food supplies, leaving the family in a precarious situation. However,

Barnabus Jones Farm. *Author's collection.*

the Jones children, displaying remarkable courage, managed to save a small stash of country hams. While the soldiers searched the buildings, the children sat on top of the hams in a box, preventing the soldiers from discovering them. This small act of defiance ensured that the family had some food left after the troops moved on. Tragically, the farm next door was not so fortunate—it was completely burned to the ground by Sherman's troops, a loss that highlighted the devastation wreaked by the war on local communities.

Despite these hardships, Barnabus Jones continued to farm the land, raising his family and maintaining the farm's productivity. Barnabus and eight other members of the Jones family are buried at the family cemetery, which still exists today across Penny Road from the original farmstead. This cemetery stands as a reminder of the family's enduring presence in the region, as well as their contributions to the development of Cary.

By the mid-twentieth century, however, the once vibrant agricultural landscape of Wake County had begun to change. As suburbanization spread, the rural farms that had defined the area for generations faced increasing pressure from developers eager to transform the land into residential neighborhoods. In 1957, A.J. Bartley, an economics professor at North

Carolina State University, purchased the Barnabus Jones farm. Bartley, who had a deep love for farming, revitalized the property, continuing its agricultural legacy while also working to preserve the historical and natural character of the land.

Bartley's stewardship was crucial in maintaining the farm's rural identity in the face of rapid urbanization. He resisted pressure from developers who sought to turn the surrounding tobacco farms into residential communities. While many nearby farms were sold and transformed into suburban developments, Bartley's efforts ensured that the Jones farm remained intact, continuing to serve as a living testament to the region's agricultural past.

Under Bartley's care, the farm continued to thrive as an active operation, with Bartley preserving not only the land but also the legacy of the Jones family. His efforts were instrumental in maintaining the land as a piece of local history, standing as a reminder of the struggles and triumphs of those who had worked it for more than a century. When the land was eventually sold to the Town of Cary in 2000, it marked the end of an era.

Although the land was no longer privately held, the purchase by the town ensured that this historically significant property would be preserved for future generations. As part of the sale agreement, Bartley retained a small portion of the land as a life estate, allowing him to continue living on the property until his death. This arrangement helped maintain a physical connection to the past, even as the surrounding area became increasingly urbanized.

Today, the land that was once the Barnabus Jones farm is a part of Cary's rapidly developing urban landscape. However, the historical significance and core features of the property have been preserved so the history can still be witnessed by those who take the time to find it. The original homestead, schoolhouse and slave quarters, though weathered by time, stand as reminders of the farm's past. These structures, along with the 3.3 acres of preserved land, provide a window into the daily lives of those who lived and worked there more than two centuries ago.

Barnabas Jones Farm, also known as the Bartley Farm, serves as a hidden piece of living history, a place where enduring connection to the land can be seen, felt and appreciated through the buildings that remain and trees that still fruit today.

To visit this preserved piece of history, go to Jack Smith Park at 9725 Penny Road. From the parking lot at the children's playground and splash pad, walk to the opposite side of the lot from the playground along the path that leads into the woods. The path will emerge at the site of the historic Barnabas Jones Farm.

Cary Prison Farm

Beneath the familiar grounds of the North Carolina State Fairgrounds and the cultural enrichment of the North Carolina Museum of Art lies the hidden history of the Cary Prison Farm. It played a significant role in North Carolina's history, evolving through military, agricultural and correctional uses over nearly eight decades. Spanning approximately 2,600 acres in its prime, the land's history reflects broader societal shifts in military strategy, agriculture and corrections.

Before becoming a correctional facility, the land that would house the Cary Prison Farm held strategic and agricultural importance. During the Civil War, the area hosted military encampments. As the years passed, the land continued to serve agricultural purposes, owned by various individuals and families.

In August 1918, the federal government leased between sixteen thousand and twenty-two thousand acres, including this property, to establish Camp Polk as part of the U.S. military's World War I efforts. Named after Revolutionary War officer and Raleigh resident William Polk, Camp Polk was intended to be a tank training facility. Temporary bunkhouses and stables were erected for civilian workers, but construction halted when the war ended in November 1918. The U.S. Army abandoned the site in early 1919.

With the cessation of military use, North Carolina's State Prison purchased 2,600 acres of Camp Polk's land in 1920 to establish a prison farm. The bunkhouses left by the army were repurposed to house inmates, marking the beginning of the site's transformation into a correctional institution. Critics, including Caryite J.M. Templeton Jr., voiced concerns about its proximity to the growing town of Cary, citing the stigma of housing inmates nearby and its removal of prime agricultural land from productive civilian use, stating in the *Raleigh Times* in 1919:

> *Some of the people of Cary community are unable to reconcile the professions of neighborliness on the part of the Raleigh Chamber of Commerce and the part of the chamber is playing in locating the State Prison Farm on what is reliably reported as the contemplated location, i.e, from the Tucker farm to the E.J. Bagwell farm, fronting about three-fourths of a mile on the Cary-*

> *Raleigh highway, and extending back northwest to include three thousand acres....It largely withdraws from productive industry a large body of good land in an excellent location...inmates are undesirable as neighbors.... The people of Cary and the suburban section affected are making a great sacrifice for the development of the threatened section.*

Regardless, the Cary Prison Farm became fully operational by the early 1920s. Its primary aim was agricultural self-sufficiency, producing crops to feed inmates and generating revenue through surplus sales. By 1923, new brick and steel buildings had replaced the temporary structures, designed to house two hundred inmates securely.

Throughout its early years, the Cary Prison Farm was praised for its agricultural efficiency and sanitary conditions. Sanitation scores ranged from 81 percent in 1921 to an impressive 98 percent in 1924. The name change to Camp Polk Farm in the 1930s, further distanced the institution from its penal affiliation.

Initially, the farm housed African American male inmates, reflecting the segregated correctional system of the time. By 1930, white inmates had been added, although the facility reverted to being all–African American in the 1940s. Integration occurred in 1956, albeit partially, mirroring the gradual societal changes in race relations.

By the 1950s, the prison's focus had begun shifting from farming to vocational training and industrial work. This pivot was fueled partly by economic considerations and changing correctional philosophies. Despite these efforts, issues of inmate escapes and subsequent crimes plagued the facility, exacerbating local opposition. Additionally, the land was becoming increasingly valuable.

In March 1956, Governor Luther Hodges proposed relocating Polk Prison to a site farther from Raleigh, citing the increasing value of the Cary property. In a memorandum to Prison Department Director W.F. Bailey, Hodges remarked, "I would be hopeful we could get the farm a little further away, and we can make a lot of money in the years ahead with the Cary property and still get our work done as well, don't you think?"

Bailey responded in agreement, noting the potential benefits of moving the farming and dairy operations to a more suitable location. He acknowledged that the land's value had grown too high for its current purpose and suggested that the area could instead support industrial expansion. According to Bailey, such a move would not only create an additional income stream for the prison system but also provide vocational and rehabilitation programs for inmates who could not be assigned to Central Prison due to its maximum-security designation. Bailey added that some facilities under construction at Polk Farm were already aligned with this vision. He suggested that land could be designated for industrial programs, with the surplus acreage sold off for revenue.

While Bailey endorsed this new direction for Polk Prison, Hodges remained hesitant about allocating significant state funds to the site. In December 1956, Hodges reiterated his concerns, writing to Bailey, "I seriously question spending any more capital money at Polk. Why don't we pick another spot?"

Two high-profile incidents in the late 1950s highlighted the challenges of managing an adult prison near a residential area. In 1959, a recently released inmate murdered Raleigh businessman Trent Ragland. The following year, escapee Robert Tyson committed multiple violent crimes, including murder and rape, sparking widespread public outcry. These incidents prompted Governor Terry Sanford, elected in 1961, to support transforming the prison into a youth-focused rehabilitation center.

In December 1963, Polk Youth Center was established as a vocational and educational training facility for young male offenders. This shift aligned with contemporary trends emphasizing rehabilitation over punishment.

Despite its rehabilitative mission, Polk Youth Center struggled to meet its ideals. By the 1990s, overcrowding, violence and reports of sexual crimes highlighted the center's limitations. Recognizing these shortcomings, the state legislature funded the construction of a new facility in Butner, Granville County. In 1997, Polk Youth Center officially relocated, leaving the original Cary site vacant.

The original Cary Prison Farm encompassed much of what is now the North Carolina State Fairgrounds and nearby areas. Over time, the state sold off portions of the land to meet other needs. By the late 1950s, the property had been reduced to 557 acres, illustrating the gradual urbanization and changing priorities of the region.

In July 2000, the North Carolina General Assembly transferred the former Polk Youth Center property to the Department of Cultural Resources for use by the North Carolina Museum of Art. This marked a new chapter for the land, transitioning from a site of confinement to one of cultural enrichment.

The history of the Cary Prison Farm is further enriched by the personal stories of inmates, documented by journalist Mary Hicks Hamilton. Her interviews with more than two hundred inmates provided unique insights into their lives, lending a human perspective to the facility's history. Her articles in the *Raleigh News & Observer* during the 1950s reflected the broader cultural and social dynamics of the era.

The original Cary Prison Farm, now lost beneath the modern State Fairgrounds, stands as a testament to shifting correctional philosophies, evolving community development pressures and broader societal changes. From its Civil War encampments and World War I training facilities to its transformation into a state prison farm, a youth rehabilitation center and to its ultimate use today as the State Fairgrounds and the North Carolina Museum of Art, the land tells a layered history of societal change. Although its physical traces have vanished, the legacy of the Cary Prison Farm stands as a poignant reminder that history often lies hidden beneath modern landmarks, which themselves may one day become tomorrow's hidden history.

THE RAILROAD LEGACY

Cary's development is closely tied to its early railroad history, a narrative deeply interwoven with the town's founding and growth. The enduring presence of the railroad, with its sights and sounds woven into Cary's landscape even today, symbolizes the foundation on which the town was built. It was the railroad that drew Frank Page to the area, catalyzing Cary's transformation. For generations, the whistle of the train has marked the town's rhythm, signaling arrivals, departures and the significant historical events that unfolded along its tracks.

The mid-nineteenth century marked a pivotal moment in Cary's history, defined by the arrival of two transformative developments: its founder, Frank Page, and the construction of the North Carolina Railroad. In 1854, the state-owned North Carolina Railroad laid tracks through the area, selecting Cary's relatively flat and dry topography as part of its route connecting Goldsboro to Charlotte. These tracks, constructed primarily through enslaved labor, would become a cornerstone of Cary's identity. This railroad remains the northernmost track in Cary today.

In 1868, Cary saw the arrival of a second railroad, the Chatham Railroad, which extended from Raleigh to the coal fields of Chatham County. By late 1867, regular passenger service had begun in Cary, paving the way for an economic surge. By the time the town was officially incorporated on April 3, 1871, the Chatham Railroad had established a warehouse that doubled as a passenger waiting room. The town's physical boundaries were defined as a one-square-mile radius measured from this railroad warehouse—a testament to how integral railroads were to Cary's identity.

The junction of these two railroads catalyzed Cary's first period of growth. Frank Page recognized the opportunity presented by this convergence of rail lines. In 1869, Page purchased three hundred acres on both sides of the tracks for $2,000. Among Page's ventures was the construction of a hotel near the railroads to accommodate the passengers. This hotel, now the Page-Walker Arts & History Center, became an iconic structure with its elegant French Second Empire architecture—an unusual sight in the rural South.

The combination of the North Carolina and Chatham Railroads positioned Cary as a hub for travelers and commerce. By 1880, Cary had grown to a modest population of 316. The railroads not only shaped the town's geography but also its economy, serving as a conduit for goods, mail and passengers. Stories from the time illustrate how the railroads became part of the daily lives of residents.

Esther Ivey, born in 1890, recounted vivid memories of life along the railroads to various sources throughout the years. One story she told often was about the train races. In the early 1900s, when she was just a teenager, she, like many others would take the train into Raleigh for entertainment and shopping. Upon returning, Cary passengers would divide on each of the trains on the separate tracks. As the trains ran parallel to Cary, Miss Ivey reported that passengers would throw open their window shouting for their engineer to go faster to beat the other train to Cary. She recalled the laughter and the shouting as embers from the train would enter through the windows.

As trains entered Cary, a switchman stationed in a two-story tower managed the critical task of operating the track switches to direct the lead train safely through the crossing. This junction at Cary, known to railroad crews as Fetner, was locally pronounced as "Feetner." The name honored W.H. Fetner, a distinguished engineer from Hamlet, North Carolina, who worked for the Seaboard Air Line Railroad. Over his remarkable fifty-year career, Fetner achieved the rare feat of never having his engine derail. To honor his dedication and exceptional service, Seaboard established a station at the southern end of its double track near Cary, naming it after him. The railroad section controlled by the switchman ran from Raleigh, passed through Cary and ended in Mr. Fetner's hometown of Hamlet. Some accounts from the time describe how the operator in the

Fetner tower had to determine which racing train would reach the crossing first and quickly switch the track in its favor. Alarmed by the speed of the approaching trains, he would sometimes make the switch and then leap from the two-story tower, fearing a derailment as the trains sped into the curve approaching Cary.

During both the Civil War and World War I, the emotional connection Cary residents had with the railroad—often serving as a link to the larger world and the harsh realities of war—was evident. Residents like Miss Esther Ivey often recalled gathering by the tracks to watch troop trains pass through and waving or to accompany Cary departing soldiers as they caught the train to join the war effort. During this time, the downtown church bells would ring at noon daily as a reminder to Cary residents to stop and pray for our troops.

Like much of the United States, Cary was hit hard by the Great Depression. The economic downturn brought significant challenges to the town, including the failure of the Bank of Cary in 1931 and municipal bankruptcy by October 1932. The financial strain led to rapid turnover in leadership, with four mayors serving within two years. In 1937, the mayor, town clerk and police chief all resigned—a clear sign of Cary's struggles.

The Depression also marked the decline of railroads in the region. The Durham and Southern Railroad, which had connected Apex and Durham since the late 1800s, ceased passenger service during this period.

Cary train depot. *Page-Walker Arts and History Center/Leslie Douglas.*

Carpenter Village, in northwest Cary, lost its depot, and the building was demolished in the ensuing years. Advances in steam engine technology and the rise of automobiles and other transportation methods made some rail services obsolete.

The original Cary train depot, which had been a fixture in the town for more than a century, was torn down in the 1970s. A new station, Cary Station at 211 North Academy Street, was built in 1996, honoring the town's railroad heritage while accommodating modern needs. A new transportation hub to further modernize and expand local train service is currently in development at that location in downtown Cary.

The often hidden history of Cary's railroads is more than just a timeline of construction and technological advancements. It's a story of community, resilience and transformation. From being the location where Cary's Civil War casualties would be delivered to the junction of two rail lines in the nineteenth century and the memories of soldiers departing during World War I, as well as the site of local revelry of the train races, the railroads have been interwoven with the town's identity.

Today, the Page-Walker Arts & History Center stands as the only remaining testament to Frank Page's vision and the foundational role of railroads in Cary's story outside of the tracks themselves. Although the Fetner switch tower is no longer standing, the Fetner station sign remains, albeit somewhat hidden. It can still be seen from the fence line in front of the Page-Walker, looking left toward the notorious curve in the tracks. Today, the sound of the train whistle, a timeless herald, is still heard a few times daily as the train approaches Cary—a familiar sound that has echoed through the town for centuries.

North Carolina's First Paved Road: Chatham Street

In 1919, the State Highway Commission was restructured, allowing its new leaders to expand North Carolina's involvement in road construction. Frank Page, son of Cary's founder, was appointed to lead the commission. Under his leadership, a significant $50 million bond issued in 1921 enabled the construction of nearly five thousand miles of highways across the state. Over his ten-year tenure, North Carolina earned the nickname the "Good Roads State." Frank's achievements led to his appointment by President Hoover as chairman of the National

Town of Cary Boasts N.C.'s First Paved Road

The Town of Cary has many firsts to its credit, but one which changed the entire complexion of the Wake County community was a paved road, believed to be the first in North Carolina.

The town's beginnings centered around the railroads. At one time, as many as 60 trains a day passed through the growing hamlet. Now, few people earn their livelihood from railroading.

The advent of paved roads and the beginning of the end of railroading in Cary came about nearly at the same time. It was in 1917 that the General Assembly created a special, one-mile-wide road district. People living in the district voted for bonds to build the road.

However, it would seem that not all residents in the road district were for the paved road as the vote was very close and the bond election was finally determined by the courts.

The old dirt road from Cary to Raleigh wasn't the best road in North Carolina in the late teens. It twisted and curved around and crossed the railroad tracks no less than five or six times on the short hop to the capital city.

The original plan called for the new road to have a straight run into Raleigh along the south side of the railroad tracks. Then an influential Negro merchant of Method, Berry O'Kelly, got the plan changed so the road would come past his business.

The plan called for the paved road to cross the railroad tracks west of the fairgrounds, go past O'Kelly's store and tie into Hillsborough Street in Raleigh.

Cary citizenry had a second occasion to celebrate a paved road just a few years later when the road between Apex and Cary was completed. The road eventually became part of U.S. 1. Millions of visitors came through Cary and the town changed during the 1920s from a railroad town to an automobile town.

Interesting Old Will Frees Some Slaves

By TOM BYRD
Special Correspondent

Colonel Fred Olds, the late Raleigh historian, called it one of Wake County's strangest and most interesting wills.

He was referring to the will of Nathaniel Jones, whose plantation, White Plains, once extended for miles on the east side of what is now Cary.

But more interesting than the size of his estate was Jones' views on the fundamental rights of man, which he used as an argument against slavery.

In fact, he begins his will by stating:

"First, my will is that all my negroes, male and female, who have arrived at the age of 24 years . . . be emancipated or liberated, whenever the laws of the state of North Carolina will admit or tolerate it. . ."

"I suppose it will be asked what are my reasons for emancipating my Negro slaves when the laws of the state will not admit it," he wrote.

The laws of North Carolina in 1815 did not permit slaves to be set free. Nor would they be freed until the Civil War a half century later. Ironically, two of Jones' grandsons would die in the Civil War, both of whom were named Nathaniel Jones.

Above: West Chatham Street, 1928. *Page-Walker Arts and History Center/Leslie Douglas.*

Left: Cary boasted the first North Carolina paved road. *From the* News and Observer, *April 18, 1971.*

Highway Safety Council. After retiring from public service, he became a prominent vice-president and influential leader at Wachovia Bank.

One of the commission's early milestones was the completion of North Carolina's first paved road in 1920, now known as Chatham Street in Cary. Originally called the Western Wake Highway, this road significantly improved travel between Raleigh and Cary. As commuting became easier, more Cary residents worked in Raleigh, and some Raleigh workers chose to move to Cary. This shift fueled Cary's residential development, with the town's population growing by 64 percent during the 1920s.

Interestingly, Frank's brother, Ambassador Walter Hines Page, has a thread in this history, given his pivotal role during World War I. After his death in 1918, the ambassador was celebrated as a national hero for his diplomatic efforts that helped bring the war to an end. His grave, located at Old Bethesda Cemetery in Aberdeen, North Carolina, became a site of pilgrimage for grateful Americans who wished to honor his legacy. The influx of visitors created a demand for better access to the cemetery. Initially, Frank Page resisted using state resources to build a road to the site, wanting to avoid any appearance of favoritism. However, public sentiment eventually led to the construction of a road to accommodate the increasing traffic.

Cary's role as the home of North Carolina's first paved road and Cary's founding family's contributions to establishing the state as the Good Roads State is a lesser-known yet significant part of Cary history that deserves recognition and celebration. This connection to Cary's history is particularly meaningful to me because my uncle, Brown Loflin, was appointed to the North Carolina Highway Commission in 1973. During his tenure, he became a celebrated member and County Commissioner, earning several Long Leaf Pine Awards for his contributions, including his work in establishing North Carolina's roadways, and the creation of the Denton Farm Park.

Hidden Natural Treasures

Beneath its modern landscape lies a hidden natural legacy that few know but is easily accessible. Among Cary's most surprising features is a small but thriving redwood forest, a rare and unexpected gem in the heart of the South. In addition to these towering ancient trees, Cary is home to a variety of other unique natural elements, from unusual tree species to distinctive plant life, each with its own fascinating story, creating one of North Carolina's few state nature preserves. These natural wonders stand quietly among Cary's modern bustle, waiting to be discovered.

Hidden Unique Redwood Tree Grove in Downtown Cary

Remarkable hidden history lives behind the town hall in downtown in the form of an unusual grove of dawn redwoods. This miniature redwood forest, often overlooked by passersby, is not only a striking feature of the landscape but also a vital reminder of conservation efforts and the interconnectedness of our ecosystem in Cary.

Dawn redwoods are an ancient species that once thrived across the northern hemisphere. However, by the end of the last ice age, they were thought to be extinct in the wild. For nearly 2 million years, these trees disappeared from Earth's landscape, until a remarkable discovery occurred in the 1940s. A small grove of living dawn redwoods was found in central

China, specifically in the Sichuan and Hubei Provinces. This discovery was groundbreaking, as paleobotanists had believed the species to be extinct.

Following this discovery, Harvard University organized expeditions to collect seeds from the Chinese groves. The seeds were distributed to botanical gardens and responsible land users across the globe, including in the United States. The introduction of these seeds allowed for the propagation of dawn redwoods in various parts of the world, including North Carolina.

In 2000, during an expansion project for the town hall, Cary planted a small grove of these remarkable trees based on their suitability for the steep hillside behind the public safety wing of the town hall. With fifteen trees planted in a carefully designed landscape, the grove quickly became one of the densest collections of dawn redwoods in North Carolina. Each tree has grown to more than forty-five feet tall, although they remain relatively small compared to their potential height of more than one hundred feet in ideal conditions.

The redwoods in downtown Cary hold significant ecological, educational and cultural importance. As members of the *Metasequoia* genus, these trees are not only an essential part of the ecosystem but also play a crucial role in climate change mitigation. With their capacity to absorb large amounts of carbon dioxide, dawn redwoods contribute to improving air quality and combating global warming.

Moreover, the grove provides critical habitat for local wildlife. Birds, insects and other small creatures thrive in the underbrush and the canopy created by the trees, promoting biodiversity in an otherwise urban environment. The presence of such a diverse ecosystem in downtown Cary emphasizes the importance of integrating natural spaces within an ever growing urban development.

The historical significance of the grove cannot be overlooked either. The fact that these trees represent a species once believed to be extinct highlights the resilience of nature and the importance of conservation efforts. By planting these trees, Cary has contributed to the preservation of a species that has endured the tests of time.

As Cary continues to grow, the importance of preserving natural spaces like the redwood grove cannot be overstated. Urban development poses threats to local ecosystems, making it crucial for communities to prioritize conservation. Cary's commitment to maintaining the health of the grove is vital for ensuring its longevity and the continued benefits it provides. Discover the hidden redwood forest for yourself today. This magical spot lives on Wilkinson Avenue, between the town hall and the Herb Young Community Center.

HEMLOCK BLUFFS NATURE PRESERVE

Hemlock Bluffs Nature Preserve, a hidden treasure in Cary located at 2616 Kildaire Farm Road, is a captivating remnant of an ancient era. This 140-acre preserve is home to a rare microhabitat where eastern hemlock trees (*Tsuga canadensis*) thrive far from their typical range in the Appalachian Mountains. Their presence, along with a diverse ecosystem of plants and wildlife unique to the area, offers a glimpse into a time when glaciers dominated the landscape.

More than ten thousand years ago, glaciers covered much of North America, including the Cary area. As the glaciers receded, they left behind a rare collection of north-facing bluffs that receive little sunlight. These shaded slopes maintain cool, moist conditions that mimic the environment of higher elevations, allowing species like eastern hemlocks to survive even as the climate warmed. Today, these majestic trees—some hundreds of years old—stand as a testament to this ancient history, their nearest relatives found more than two hundred miles west in the Appalachian foothills.

The history of Hemlock Bluffs' preservation began in 1961, when the National Park Service recognized its ecological significance. Despite this early acknowledgment, it wasn't until 1976 that the State of North Carolina purchased eighty-five acres of the land from Cary developer Jefferson Sugg, thanks to advocacy by a group now known as Friends of Hemlock Bluffs. In 1979, the land became a State Nature and Historic Preserve, included in the State Registry of Natural Heritage Areas. Still, the land lacked proper funding and stewardship to become a protected nature preserve. Hemlock Bluffs faced significant threat issues ranging from littering and poaching of hemlock seedlings and rare plants to unauthorized activities like nighttime drinking parties and repelling down the bluffs and even a devastating 100,000-gallon sewage spill in Swift Creek that meandered through the land. Ultimately, these events highlighted the vulnerability of this unique habitat.

Despite initial tensions between local conservation groups, encroaching development, the state and the Town of Cary, a greater commitment to stewardship and collaboration resulted. The town took over oversight of the land in the early 1980s. Cary developer Tim Smith purchased 30 acres adjacent to the bluffs and donated it to the town. Colonel William Walton Stevens owned a 50-acre tract of adjacent land, but no funds could be raised for their purchase. When the 560-acre Regency Park development began in 1982, Edward Woolner, Regency Park developer, bought the

Stevens property and donated 32 acres of it to the town to complete the 140-acre preserve.

Colonel Stevens and his wife, Emily, generously donated $50,000 toward the construction of the nature center at the heart of Hemlock Bluffs. The aptly named Stevens Nature Center opened in 1992 and serves as a gateway for visitors to learn about the preserve's unique ecosystem.

Hemlock Bluffs features more than four miles of trails, carefully designed to minimize human impact on the delicate ecosystem. Two main trail systems provide visitors with contrasting experiences of the preserve's uplands and floodplain:

- Chestnut Oak Trail and Beech Tree Cove Trail: These upland loops wind through dry hills populated by chestnut oaks, longleaf pines and beech trees. Visitors can explore geological features such as the eighty-foot bluffs, which mark an ancient fault line created 220 million years ago. Controlled burns are periodically conducted here to maintain the health of the ecosystem.
- Swift Creek Loop Trail: This floodplain trail descends one hundred stairs to reach the creek, offering views of tulip trees, hollies and an extensive stand of bamboo-like cane. Along the way, hikers may spot heartleaf, trout lilies and pipsissewa.

Boardwalks and wooden overlooks provide stunning views of the hemlocks and Swift Creek, creating the feeling of being in the mountains in south Cary. As R. Wayne Mingis, Cary's former recreation director, remarked at the preserve's opening, "People in this area no longer have to drive to the mountains. They can go to Hemlock Bluffs and enjoy the same effect."

Hemlock Bluffs is not just about the trees. It is a sanctuary for an incredible array of flora and fauna. The preserve supports rare Appalachian species such as galax, yellow lady's slipper orchids and five moss species not usually found outside the Appalachian region. In the uplands, salamanders—including marbled, spotted and dwarf species—breed in seasonal pools. Swift Creek, which runs through the preserve, harbors rare freshwater mussels, madtom fish and even a newly discovered crayfish species. The birdlife is equally remarkable, with 130 species recorded, including the distinctive barred owl. Nest boxes are commonly found around the preserve to provide habitats for owls and other birds.

Today, strict rules ensure the preserve's integrity. Visitors must stay on designated trails, and collecting plants or animals is strictly prohibited. These measures, combined with ongoing conservation efforts, help safeguard Hemlock Bluffs for future generations.

Hemlock Bluffs provides a way for people of all ages to connect with nature and this unique remnant of the ice age. For families, the nature-themed play area near the Stevens Nature Center offers a whimsical space where children can explore oversized mushrooms, balance on logs and climb through tunnels. For adults, educational programs and guided hikes provide deeper insights into the preserve's ecological and geological wonders. Seasonal events, such as controlled burns and wildlife observations, offer opportunities to witness the dynamic processes that shape this unique environment.

Hemlock Bluffs stands as a testament to the power of preservation and community effort. From its origins as a glacial relic to its current status as a treasured public space, the preserve encapsulates the delicate balance between human activity and natural heritage. In a rapidly growing region, Hemlock Bluffs Nature Preserve remains a serene refuge, offering visitors a rare chance to step back in time and marvel at nature as it once was and still is inside this hidden gem of Cary.

Hidden History Treasures?

High House

Earlier in the book, the history of the long-gone High House and its Revolutionary War–era origins was explored, along with the intriguing lore connected to the property now part of the Black Creek Greenway. The legend of hidden treasure buried on the land continues to captivate treasure hunters, even though the property is now owned by the Town of Cary. Visitors to the greenway are required to stay on the paved path, as specified by the greenway's rules. This continued interest in the site reflects the enduring mystery and allure of the land at the intersection of High House and Northwest Maynard Roads.

As review, High House, originally perched on a hill near what is now High House Road, was a grand home known for its height—one of the tallest buildings in the region when it was built sometime in the 1760s by Tignall Jones. His descendant Leander Williams was born there in 1883. After moving away, Leander Williams had a vivid dream of treasure buried beneath the fireplace hearth of the old High House. He told his mother about the dream, finding out that she had the same dream. Eager to investigate, they rushed back to the house, only to find that the hearth had been recently dismantled, leaving the mystery unresolved. This strange coincidence added to the lore surrounding the house, further fueling local speculation about hidden riches.

Over the years, this belief grew stronger, particularly as rumors circulated about strange occurrences and the house's eventual demise. According to one version of the story, a group of boys, attempting to smoke out a beehive from the house's walls, accidentally set the structure on fire. As the house burned, many locals started digging through its walls and embers, eager to find the rumored riches.

Beyond the treasure itself, the mystery deepened with reports of ghostly apparitions associated with High House. The house was said to be haunted by spirits, perhaps tied to the people who had frequented the site in search of the elusive treasure. There is also a history of sudden madness and tragic events that befell families who lived on the property before the town acquired it. The most enduring ghost story is that of a young woman who was killed there during the property's time as a local horse racing spot. Caught in a love triangle, she was murdered by one of her jealous suitors. Leander Williams, who grew up on the property, and others in the family reported seeing a female spirit there throughout his childhood and into adulthood—one he believed to be the ghost of this woman.

Today, High House is no longer standing, but its legend lives on in Cary's history. Tales of hidden treasure, a turncoat owner dating back to the Revolutionary War and the haunting stories of the house and land that continue through generations secure the location as one of the most captivating in Cary's local lore and history.

H. Charles Beil's Hidden Treasure in Cary: Theodosia's Lost Legacy

While doing research for this book, I received a message from someone who wished to stay anonymous that simply asked, "Do you know about the hidden treasure in Cary?" Immediately, I thought they were referring to the High House legend of the lost buried treasure in the house's hearth. But as I looked closer at the included, expertly layered historical map and a modern-day map that a North Carolina engineer firm completed, I realized they were talking about something completely different and began to investigate further.

In the shadowy world of treasure hunting, few names carry as much intrigue as H. Charles Beil, known to many simply as the "Treasure Man." Across the American landscape, Beil hid dozens of treasure caches, tantalizing explorers with the promise of riches. The rules are simple: find it and the treasure is yours. These caches, ranging in difficulty from mildly challenging to maddeningly cryptic, have drawn hundreds of treasure hunters into the fray. One of the most captivating is "Theodosia's cache," which holds material wealth in the context of the mysterious story of real-life historical figure Theodosia Burr Alston.

Theodosia Burr Alston, born in 1783, was the beloved daughter of Aaron Burr, the controversial third vice president of the United States. Her father doted on her, nurturing her intelligence and providing an education rare for women of her time. She would go on to marry Joseph Alston, a wealthy South Carolina plantation owner and later the state's governor during the War of 1812. Yet despite her privileged life, tragedy seemed to haunt Theodosia.

By the winter of 1812, Theodosia's life had unraveled. Her young son had died, and her father was living in exile after his infamous duel with Alexander Hamilton. It was in this somber state that she boarded the ship *Patriot* on December 31, 1812, bound for New York. Theodosia was hoping to reunite with her father after his return to the United States. The *Patriot*, however, never reached its destination. The ship and all aboard it vanished without a trace, spawning one of the most persistent mysteries of early America.

Over the years, many theories have emerged about the fate of Theodosia. Some say that the *Patriot* was caught in a violent storm, while others suggest that it fell victim to a pirate attack. It is this latter version of the story that has fascinated treasure hunters for more than a century…and it is the story that the Treasure Man weaved into his hidden cache.

According to one version of the pirate legend, Theodosia's ship was overtaken by a notorious band of pirates off the coast of North Carolina. Among them was a pirate named Old Frank Burdick. On his deathbed, Burdick reportedly confessed to being involved in the attack. He claimed that Theodosia and all aboard the *Patriot* were murdered and that their belongings—including her fabled jewels—were divided among the pirates. Haunted by Theodosia's image, Burdick allegedly buried his share of the plunder somewhere along a prominent inland trail. This pirate's hoard—coins and jewels long lost to the wilds of North Carolina—forms the basis of Theodosia's cache.

Theodosia's cache, hidden by the Treasure Man in 2016, begins its trail near the coast of North Carolina, around the famed Outer Banks. This rugged region, steeped in shipwreck lore and pirate history, is a fitting starting point for the hunt. The treasure is marked as a "one-skull" difficulty—relatively easy by the Treasure Man's standards—but the path to the cache is still shrouded in mystery. The only tools provided are a cryptic map and a PDF story chronicling the legend of Theodosia's final days.

The map, though simple in appearance, is anything but straightforward. The markings, obscure symbols and fragmented text make it clear that knowledge of local history—and the nuances of Theodosia's life—may be crucial in deciphering its meaning. The map seemingly tracks Burdick's movement inland, taking treasure hunters on a journey from the salt-swept shores of the Atlantic to the wild interior of North Carolina. And that journey has led many treasure seekers to believe that the cache may be hidden somewhere near—or in—Cary, North Carolina.

Jason Griffin and his wife were two such explorers. Having previously searched for one of the Treasure Man's Virginia caches, they turned their attention to the Theodosia cache. With the map in hand and a keen sense of adventure, they embarked on a quest to decode the cryptic clues.

Jason explained that his search for Theodosia's cache took him and his wife to the Swift Creek Nature Preserve. He was drawn to the area by clues in the PDF that referenced North Carolina landmarks, including a mention of Swift Creek. After discovering that Dobbs County and Cross Creek (now Fayetteville) were no longer recognized by modern maps, Jason cross-referenced historical documents and realized that the treasure map provided by the Treasure Man had likely been altered in an image editing program.

One particularly interesting clue was the appearance of a faint red dot and gray star on the treasure map, near Swift Creek. This clue led Jason to believe that Cary was the final resting place of the Theodosia cache. His research even uncovered a potential hiding spot at Swift Creek Nature Preserve, a public area with open access that aligned with the Treasure Man's known methods.

Jason and his wife scoured the preserve, their excitement growing as they traversed the same trails that explorers had used centuries ago. Although they didn't find the cache, Jason remained optimistic. As he explained, "The thing about these treasure hunts is you can get real close with the clues provided, but that doesn't mean you have found it. You have to have the treasure in hand before you have joined the club as a successful treasure hunter."

Theodosia's cache represents more than just a collection of coins and gemstones. It connects seekers to the history of the mysterious disappearance of Theodosia Burr Alston and the legend of the pirates who claimed her life. For adventurers like Jason Griffin and his wife, the journey is as valuable as the prize itself. The thrill of discovery, the joy of exploring hidden places and the chance to unravel a centuries-old mystery make the hunt for Theodosia's treasure an unforgettable experience.

As the Treasure Man himself would say, "The treasure is out there. Find it, and it is yours to keep." Perhaps this hidden history is still hidden in Cary today.

Community Developments

African American Land Legacy

Cary stands as a testament to cultural interconnection and resilience in African American history. Among the foundational contributors to this legacy were African American families who were never enslaved, establishing themselves in the area during the early nineteenth century, long before the Civil War. Their efforts not only shaped the town through significant community developments and neighborhoods but also set a standard for self-reliance and community empowerment.

One of Cary's most prominent families, the Evanses, trace their lineage to free African Americans and Native Americans. The family's story begins in Charles City, Virginia, in the mid- to late 1600s, with a migration to Mecklenburg County, Virginia, by the 1700s. By 1800, the Evans family had settled in Chatham County, North Carolina, before establishing roots in Cary, Wake County, in 1890.

Members of the Evans family intermarried with the remaining Tuscarora tribe in the region, forming unions grounded in love and mutual protection during tumultuous times. This interconnected heritage of African American and Native American ancestry became a defining feature of their identity and legacy.

Unlike many African Americans of their era, the Evans family were active participants in American society, securing land grants, writing wills and engaging in legal matters. These activities highlighted their autonomy and resilience. Their patriarch, Clyde Evans Sr., epitomized these values, amassing more than one thousand acres along what is now Evans Road in Cary.

The Evans family used their extensive landholdings to develop Cary while supporting the African American community. They sold and provided land plots to African Americans, including sharecroppers, offering opportunities for ownership and self-sufficiency. Clyde Evans Sr., specifically, had a dream of helping African Americans in Cary break the cycle of generational poverty through landownership and self-sufficiency. He sold home plots to African American families, often at "sacrifice prices," to give them the start that only landownership and homeownership can provide.

The values of the Evans family and later the Bailey family—faith, self-sufficiency and love of the land—extended to property development. They helped establish significant neighborhoods such as Evans Estates, Bailey's Creek and Bailey's Court. These contributions not only supported economic independence but also laid the foundation for a thriving African American community.

The Evans family played a pivotal role in advancing education and worship in Cary. In 1965, they sold land to the Wake County School System, leading to the establishment of West Cary High School, later West Cary Middle School. During segregation, the school served as a vital institution for African American students.

In 1968, the family donated land for Cary First Christian Church, which became a cornerstone for African American worship and community life. These contributions cemented their role in fostering institutions critical to Cary's growth.

Today, the Evans-Turner Cemetery on Old Apex Road in Cary serves as a resting place for the family's ancestors. This privately owned burial ground stands as a testament to their enduring legacy, preserving the unique history of a community shaped by never-enslaved African Americans and Native Americans.

Another cornerstone of Cary's early development was the Arrington family, whose members continue to shape the town's history and community. Descendants of the Arrington and Jones families remain in Cary today, contributing to institutions such as Cary First Christian Church.

The Arrington story begins with Alfred Arrington, a former enslaved person who arrived in Cary in the late 1860s, before the town's incorporation in 1871. Born into slavery as the son of a slaveholder,

Left: Alfred Arrington, the largest landowner and a prominent leader in the late 1860s. *Barbara Engram.*

Right: Arch Arrington Sr., son of Alfred Arrington and the first African American elected official as mayor in the 1920s. *Barbara Engram.*

Alfred's life reflects a complex legacy. Family accounts tell of an intention by his enslaver to keep him in the family's care, but Alfred was ultimately sold for $300, a significant amount at the time. Soon after, he was freed by his new owner, granting him the autonomy to build a life of independence.

Choosing Cary as his home, Alfred passed down a philosophy of self-reliance, emphasizing landownership, education and fiscal responsibility. His influence set the foundation for his family's future contributions to Cary's growth.

Alfred's son, Arch Arrington Sr., built on this legacy, becoming a prominent landowner and community leader. In the1920s, Arch made history as Cary's first African American elected official as mayor, a remarkable achievement during segregation. His election sparked controversy, leading his defeated opponent to leave town in protest. Arch owned significant land near what is now West Cary Middle School and, like the Evans family, extended opportunities to others by selling land plots to African Americans, fostering homeownership and economic independence.

The Arringtons held education as a central value. Alfred's grandchildren Emily Arrington Jones and Goelet Arrington donated land to Wake County Schools to establish Cary Elementary Colored School, now Kingswood Elementary School. This ensured that African American children had access to education during segregation, exemplifying the family's commitment to uplifting their community.

Arch Arrington Jr., a family leader, famously said, "No one can keep you down unless he stands there with his foot on your back holding you down. If he stands there holding you down, he will not make any progress either." This philosophy reflects the family's unwavering determination to overcome adversity and their belief in contributing meaningfully to society, both in Cary and beyond, without letting challenges become an excuse.

Miss Sallie Jones, the great-granddaughter of Alfred Arrington, exemplified her family's enduring impact. Honored with Cary's 2024 Hometown Spirit Award in November 2024, she dedicated her life to preserving the town's African American history. Miss Sallie passed away on February 14, 2025, at age one hundred, just months after receiving this deserved award.

After retiring from teaching and returning to Cary, Miss Sallie was disheartened to discover that her ancestors' graves had been lost to development. This realization inspired her to protect the cemetery at Cary First Christian Church, which dates back to 1868. Under her leadership, the cemetery was surveyed, and archaeologists identified more than 160 unmarked graves. Miss Sallie meticulously researched historical records to identify those buried there and successfully advocated for the cemetery's registration with the State of North Carolina. It became the first cemetery in Cary—and all of Wake County—to be designated a historic landmark, located at 300 West Cornwall Drive.

The stories of the Evans and Arrington families reveal a shared legacy of resilience, self-reliance and community-building. Their contributions to land development, education and faith have left an indelible mark on Cary's history. Streets, neighborhoods and landmarks such as Evans Road, Bailey's Creek and the historic cemetery at Cary First Christian Church stand as lasting tributes to their work.

Today, their descendants remain active in Cary, ensuring that the stories of these pioneering families continue to inspire. Their commitment to fostering opportunity, preserving history and building a thriving Cary serves as a testament to the power of perseverance and the enduring impact of Cary's early African American pioneers.

Veteran Hills and Russell Hills

Other community developers were influential in the creation of Cary's landscape. Russell O. Heater is another whose name is synonymous with the early development of Cary. Through visionary projects that addressed the needs of a growing postwar population, Heater not only changed the physical landscape of Cary but also left an enduring legacy as one of the town's earliest advocates for its potential. His efforts as a developer and his confidence in Cary's growth trajectory helped set the stage for the town's transformation into a thriving community.

In 1945, as World War II veterans returned home seeking stability and a fresh start, Heater identified an opportunity to support their reintegration while fostering growth in Cary. Purchasing land near the intersection of Walker and Parker Streets, he created Cary's first named subdivision, Veteran Hills. Heater constructed two new streets, Keener and Fairview, and sold lots at cost exclusively to returning veterans.

Cary cottages, 1940s. *Page-Walker Arts and History Center/Leslie Douglas.*

The first lot in Veteran Hills was purchased by former army sergeant Bill Keener, for whom one of the streets was named. The lots sold quickly, demonstrating the demand for affordable housing among veterans and solidifying the project as an early success. By tailoring his project to returning servicemen, Heater aligned his entrepreneurial goals with the needs of a generation rebuilding their lives.

Encouraged by his success with Veteran Hills, Heater embarked on a second development project southwest of downtown Cary along South Harrison Avenue. In 1949, Heater purchased thirty-five acres for $1,000 and showcased his knack for resourcefulness by selling the timber on the property for $600. Demonstrating a commitment to community development, he allocated three acres of the land for an extension of Hillcrest Cemetery.

Heater paved the streets and installed water lines, creating a modern and attractive neighborhood. The development came to be known as Russell Hills after a playful exchange with friends who asked about the progress of his "hills." Despite initial skepticism about his venture, Heater surprised many by successfully selling every lot at a profit.

Russell Hills highlighted Heater's ability to balance innovation with practicality. By investing in infrastructure and ensuring that the lots were ready for construction, Heater set a standard for future residential developments in Cary. His work on Russell Hills also underscored the importance of planning, as the neighborhood became a desirable area for new residents and a vital part of Cary's growth story.

Heater was not just a developer but also one of Cary's earliest and most enthusiastic advocates. His belief in the town's potential extended beyond his projects. In 1970, when Cary's population was around seven thousand, Heater attended a meeting of the Doghouse Club at Ashworth's Drug Store. Confident in Cary's future, he predicted that by 1980, the town's population would reach twenty thousand.

His bold statement was met with laughter and skepticism. Cary at the time was a small town, and such growth seemed improbable to many. However, Heater's prediction proved remarkably accurate. Due to Heater's developments. increasing annexation and growth, Cary's population doubled during the 1950s from 1,496 to 3,356 in 1960. Significantly, in 1965, IBM and other companies established operations at the 1959 created Research Triangle Park, which led to explosive growth for Cary. By 1980, Cary's population had grown to 21,763, surpassing even his ambitious forecast. In 2025, Cary's population stands around 191,000.

The neighborhoods Russell Heater created remain integral parts of the town that are still visible and viable today. Beyond his work in real estate, Heater's leadership was evident in various organizations, including the Methodist Church, the Boy Scouts, the Masonic Lodge and the Cary Recreation Corporation—forerunner of the Cary Swim Club. Additionally, he cared for Hillcrest Cemetery for more than twenty-five years and served on the Cary Town Council.

Heater also played an influential role in fostering Cary's historical and cultural identity. Collaborating with local artists and historians, he inspired efforts to document and celebrate the town's history. Notably, he encouraged Jerry Miller, an architectural draftsman and artist, to add narratives to his sketches of Cary's historic homes. This collaboration led to the publication of *Around and About Cary* in 1970, a quintessential book on the town's history.

Heater's house, still located at 120 Dry Avenue in downtown Cary, stands as a reminder of his enduring impact as a developer and civic leader and one of Cary's greatest champions.

MacGregor Downs: Cary's First Luxury Country Club Community

During the 1960s, Cary's population doubled, driven by the establishment of Research Triangle Park and the arrival of major companies like IBM and Chemstrand Corporation. To manage the rapid growth, Cary implemented its initial subdivision regulations in 1961 and revised its zoning ordinance and land use plan in 1963. Meanwhile, J. Gregory Poole Sr. began buying land south of Cary.

Nestled in the southern part of Cary, near the crossroads of U.S. 1 and U.S. 64, lies MacGregor Downs, Cary's first country club community. Established in the mid-twentieth century, it became one of the town's most transformative developments. This private and exclusive community was the vision of J. Gregory Poole Sr., a man who dreamed of bringing luxury and prestige to Cary.

Poole was no stranger to ambitious projects. His construction company played a key role in building the iconic Blue Ridge Parkway, showcasing his knack for transforming raw land into extraordinary spaces. In 1962, his visionary journey began when he identified a seven-hundred-acre tract along Cary's southern border with Apex. Inspired by its potential, Poole began acquiring the land piece by piece, with a clear but evolving vision for what it could become.

The first step in Poole's ambitious plan was creating a centerpiece for the development: a fifty-five-acre lake. This serene body of water became a focal point for the community, setting the stage for what was to come. As Poole's vision matured, he looked to the recently developed Country Club of North Carolina in Pinehurst for inspiration. He aspired to replicate the sense of prestige and quality that the Pinehurst project embodied, proving that Cary was ready for such refinement. The story goes that Poole even promised the golf pro at the North Carolina Country Club that if he came to work for MacGregor Downs County Club, Poole would get him his own golf tournament. So he did.

To bring his vision to life, Poole enlisted the developers behind Pinehurst's Country Club of North Carolina to design a master plan for a golf course community. Initially, the development was to be named after nearby Swift Creek, but Poole's daughter suggested a Scottish theme instead, honoring the family's name and golf's Scottish origins. The name MacGregor Downs was born, tying the community to a sense of heritage and sophistication.

On October 3, 1966, MacGregor Downs was officially incorporated. To the occasional chagrin of his business partners, Poole spared no expense in building the design that would define the community. Beyond the golf course, he developed streets, tennis courts, a clubhouse and recreational facilities, all surrounding the existing lake. This commitment to quality reflected Poole's desire to create not just a residential area but a prestigious landmark for Cary.

Initially, skeptics doubted the viability of such a project. MacGregor Downs was considered remote, far from Cary's other developing neighborhoods. Additionally, the cost of lots—ranging from $7,500 to $11,500—seemed exorbitant at the time, especially for Cary. Many questioned whether anyone would be willing to pay such prices to live in what was then a relatively unproven area.

Poole's gamble paid off. By 1982, the last of the four hundred lots had been sold, cementing MacGregor Downs as one of Cary's most successful and desirable communities. Over the years, it became home to notable figures, including North Carolina State University basketball coach Jim Valvano, famed football coach Lou Holtz and SAS founder Jim Goodnight.

MacGregor Downs' crowning achievement came in 1973, when it hosted the Liggett & Myers Open and the U.S. Match Play Championships. Golfing legend Jack Nicklaus teed off from the tenth green, just steps from Poole's condo, and personally praised Poole for the course's beauty and quality. This moment was particularly poignant, as Poole passed away just thirty days later, having realized his dream. Today, his legacy endures through a commissioned portrait that hangs in the clubhouse, a testament to his transformative vision.

The course itself continued to attract some of the biggest names in golf, including Arnold Palmer, Gary Player and Lee Trevino, further solidifying MacGregor Downs' reputation as a premier destination. The development even provided practical benefits for Cary. The town was able to install sewer lines beneath the lake, a little-known but critical improvement that supported the area's growth.

MacGregor Downs' success had a ripple effect on Cary's southern border, paving the way for other nearby upscale developments like Lochmere and Regency Park. These communities followed in MacGregor Downs' footsteps, replicating its blend of luxury living, beautiful aesthetics and recreational amenities.

Kildaire Farm: From Dairy Legacy to Cary's Most Ambitious Development

Driving down Kildaire Farm Road in Cary, North Carolina, it's hard to imagine that this bustling area—lined with homes, businesses and parks—was once part of a sprawling, one-thousand-acre working farm. The only visible remnant of its agricultural past is the cow cooling pond across from Trader Joe's—a serene spot now home to Cary's infamous geese. This pond serves as a quiet reminder of a bygone era when the land was alive with the hum of farm operations.

From the 1920s to the 1970s, Kildaire Farm was a thriving agricultural enterprise. Owned by the Kilgore family, the farm was known for its herd of Guernsey cows, which produced milk and other dairy products for Pine State Creamery. Alongside dairy production, the farm also housed thirty thousand chickens, whose eggs were distributed to local stores. Additionally, about two hundred beef cattle roamed its pastures. The farm was a cornerstone of the local economy and a symbol of Cary's rural roots.

Transforming Kildaire Farm from a working farm into one of Cary's most influential residential developments—and a model for urban planning across North Carolina—demanded a combination of bold vision and meticulous strategic planning. That vision came from Thomas F.

Kildaire Farm. *Page-Walker Historical Collection.*

Adams Jr., a local real estate attorney with a passion for innovative urban planning. Adams was inspired by the concept of preplanned communities, where residential, commercial and recreational spaces are integrated into a cohesive whole. He saw Kildaire Farm as the ideal location for Cary's—and North Carolina's—first Planned Unit Development (PUD).

Adams drew on the success of nearby MacGregor Downs, a golf course–centered community, to bolster his idea. He envisioned Kildaire Farms as a "town within a town"—a self-contained neighborhood that would include single-family homes, apartments, shopping centers, offices, schools, churches, recreational facilities and greenspaces. Unlike conventional suburban developments that relied on clear-cutting and uniform street layouts, Adams's design sought to preserve the area's natural beauty and topography.

His plan prioritized environmental harmony. Natural tree canopies would remain intact, drainage systems would use natural waterways rather than curbs and gutters where possible and backyards would blend into greenspaces. Streets were designed to follow the land's natural curves, creating medians and slowing traffic. Tennis courts were strategically placed on hills to catch cooling breezes. This thoughtful approach earned praise, with the *Cary News* calling it "development gone sane."

Convincing the Kilgore heirs, who owned Kildaire Farm at the time, to sell their property for this ambitious project was no small feat. Adams presented his plan as a revolutionary concept that would not only transform Cary but also set a precedent for future developments. His vision of a balanced, sustainable community with diverse amenities resonated with the heirs, and they agreed to sell.

Adams worked closely with Cary town leadership to adopt the PUD model for this project and encouraged them to consider it for future developments. Kildaire Farms would serve as a test case, showcasing the benefits of this innovative planning approach.

The grand opening of Kildaire Farms in 1974 marked the beginning of an exciting new chapter for Cary. However, the recession of 1974–75 brought the housing market to a near standstill, halting the momentum of the project. Financial challenges forced Adams to sell the development.

The project found new life when two prominent figures—Walter Davis, a North Carolina native and oil tycoon, and James Harrington, a developer and North Carolina secretary of transportation—purchased the development. Their involvement helped stabilize the project, although financial hurdles continued to arise over the years.

Despite these challenges, the core principles of the PUD design remained resilient. The development stayed true to Adams's original vision, maintaining its emphasis on environmental preservation and community-focused planning.

Between 1979 and 1992, twenty-two additional PUDs were approved in Cary, making the town a leader in this innovative approach to urban development. No other municipality in North Carolina embraced PUDs or PUD-inspired communities on the same scale during this period. The village-style concept foundational to PUDs fostered a sense of belonging and individual communities that continues to define Cary today.

A drive down Kildaire Farm Road reveals the enduring impact of this planning model. Rather than generic subdivisions, the road is flanked by distinct neighborhoods, each with its own character—consider Kildaire

Farms, Lochmere, Regency Park, Wimbledon and more. These communities stand as a testament to the vision that transformed farmland into a thriving residential hub.

While the development of Kildaire Farms set the stage for Cary's growth and influenced urban planning across the state, the history behind it is less well known and is a story worth knowing. The transition from a one-thousand-acre farm to a model for sustainable, planned communities is a story of vision, resilience and innovation. Today, as residents enjoy those tree-lined streets, interconnected greenways and vibrant neighborhoods, they are walking through the legacy of a groundbreaking idea that turned a dairy farm into one of North Carolina's most influential developments.

The Historic Homes of Academy Street

Many people may not realize that downtown Cary is a designated historic district. The district is bounded by South Academy Street, South Harrison Avenue, West Park Street, Dry Avenue and a portion of Faculty Avenue. It was added to the National Register of Historic Places in 2001, encompassing eighteen acres and featuring more than thirty contributing historic buildings and homes. Notable landmarks like Cary High School, now the Cary Arts Center, and the Sams-Jones House—once home to Solomon Pool in an earlier version of the structure—have been highlighted. However, many other homes in the district also hold fascinating and often lesser-known histories.

Guess-Ogle House, aka the "Pink House"

Located at 215 South Academy Street, the Guess-Ogle House, affectionately known as the "Pink House," stands as a striking symbol of Cary's historical charm. Its story begins in 1830, as noted on the sign outside the home. However, the details of its original structure and its first owner remain a mystery. The State Historic Preservation Office suggests that the house may have started as a one-story, two-room dwelling in the early nineteenth century. This is particularly intriguing, as reports from 1830—twenty-four years before Frank Page's arrival—indicate that the only notable structure in the area was Bradford's Ordinary.

The mystery deepens when considering the original structure's durability. It must have been substantial, not merely a shack. When Frank Page arrived in 1856 and purchased three hundred acres of land that now forms downtown Cary (including the current location of the Pink House), the original building must have survived until at least 1880. This is when Frank likely sold a sixteen-acre parcel to his friend, Captain Harrison P. Guess, an enterprising lumberman. Captain Guess then used the existing structure as the base for his home. This suggests that whatever the original two-room structure from 1830 was, it had to have been significant enough to endure for decades.

Regardless of its origins, Captain Guess was encouraged by Frank Page to move from Orange County to Cary and establish a life with his wife, Aurelia. Shortly after their arrival in 1880, they expanded the original structure into a two-story I-house, a style popular in the post–Civil War South, with elements of Greek Revival flair.

Captain Guess became a prominent figure in early Cary. A founding member of Cary Methodist Church and a leader in the Masonic Lodge, he embodied the pioneering spirit that both Frank Page and the town of Cary were cultivating. The Guess family's legacy was further solidified when Captain Guess's daughters married into the Page family, intertwining the names of Guess and Page in Cary's history.

The house's journey didn't end with the Guess family. In 1896, Reverend John White acquired the property and introduced significant changes, including the addition of the distinctive three-story Queen Anne–style tower. This architectural addition transformed the home from a modest structure into a grand statement of ambition and vision. Reverend White, a man of both letters and faith, used the tower as a retreat where he would look out over Cary while writing his sermons.

Over the years, the house passed through multiple owners, including Mayor Waldo Rood, who ensured its preservation during Cary's mid-twentieth-century transformation. In the 1990s, Sheila and Carroll Ogle purchased the home and undertook a detailed restoration. Their efforts not only preserved the building's structural integrity but also infused it with a renewed sense of community spirit, including painting it its signature pink color. Sheila Ogle shared her personal connection to the house in her book, *The Pink House*, where the house itself is portrayed as a "character" recounting its own experiences. During their ownership, the house became a hub for community events, including holiday parties and receptions, strengthening the ties between the residents and their neighbors. Today, the home remains privately owned, preserving its historical qualities while being operated as legal offices.

The Guess-Ogle House contributes to the Cary downtown historic district and is protected by a preservation easement, ensuring that its historical significance will be maintained for future generations. It was designated a Wake County Historic Landmark in 2008. Today, the house stands as a beloved emblem of Cary's past, celebrated for its architectural beauty, thoughtful restoration and integral role in the local history. It remains a treasured gem in the heart of Cary's Downtown Historic District.

The Hunter House

Located at 311 South Academy Street, the Dr. John Pullen Hunter House holds historical importance due to its connection to Dr. Hunter and his notable family lineage. His ancestors include Isaac Hunter, who owned a well-known tavern in Wake County where the state's Constitutional Convention was held in 1788. The house itself was constructed around 1925 and received historic landmark status in 2008.

Dr. John Pullen Hunter, a prominent physician, practiced in Cary from 1920 until 1959. Dr. Hunter was also actively involved in civic life, serving on the Cary Town Board and the Wake County Board of Education, leading the Cary Chamber of Commerce and participating in the Cary Masonic Lodge. The property is also home to the district's only surviving original chicken coop. Dr. Hunter helped pay for his medical education by raising chickens and selling the eggs from this coop.

Today, the Hunter House is a standout example of well-preserved Craftsman bungalow architecture in the Downtown Historic District. The house and its adjacent chicken coop are currently undergoing historic preservation and restoration for future use as commercial restaurant spaces.

The Pasmore House

The Pasmore House, located at 307 South Academy Street in Cary, is a significant historical structure dating back to circa 1900 and is included in the National Register of Historic Places. It was built by William Pasmore for his family. Pasmore was also apparently a friend of Frank Page's, as newspaper ads dating back to 1857 list William and Frank as marketing and selling land

Above: Former Pasmore House, today's Cotton House. *Author's collection.*

Left: Pasmore House's designation sign. *Author's collection.*

Opposite, top: Front parlor of Pasmore House. *Author's collection.*

Opposite, bottom: New Downtown Cary Park. *Author's collection.*

in the area. However, shortly after building the house, William died, leaving his widow to raise their children there alone. A series of tragedies followed, resulting in the deaths of two of Pasmore children on site in 1902 and in 1906, eventually leading Mrs. Pasmore to move away from Cary.

The home has served as a boarding facility for students attending Cary High School. It was one of many boarding homes along Academy Street for Cary Academy and then Cary High School. Such homes were instrumental in accommodating students and fostering a sense of home and community

DOWNTOWN
CARY PARK
SOCIAL DISTRICT
FRANTZ

while they were away from home. The Pasmore House was a favorite among boarding students for studying given its unique pass-through fireplace on the first floor, which allowed two rooms to receive direct heat from the fireplace at once.

The house reflects the broader architectural trends of its time, particularly the Craftsman style, which gained popularity for its emphasis on handcrafted simplicity and functional beauty. Over the decades, the Pasmore House has been carefully restored to retain its historical integrity and features while incorporating modern updates. The house now serves as the home of Cotton House, blending historical preservation with contemporary community use. Visitors can experience the house's historic charm through original elements such as the exposed brick pass-through fireplace, wood floors and features such as Cary historical photographs displayed on its walls. Its more recently added back deck offers views of nearby Downtown Cary Park.

Dr. Frank W. Yarborough's House

Built around 1935 at 219 South Academy Street, Dr. Yarborough's house is a one-and-a-half-story cottage featuring simple Colonial Revival elements. The property is listed in the National Register of Historic Places.

Dr. Yarborough's two office entrances today. *Author's collection.*

Dr. Frank Yarborough was a prominent figure in Cary, both as a physician and as a community leader. He interned with Dr. J.M. Templeton, Cary's first and only doctor for many years, who brought him to Cary in the early 1900s. After Dr. Templeton's death in 1932, Dr. Yarborough continued his practice, becoming a well-respected physician in the town. His legacy also includes serving as Cary's mayor from 1927 to 1928.

Dr. Yarborough's life was marked by personal tragedy when his daughter, Mary Ray Yarborough, died from meningitis at a young age. A poignant memorial to her at Hillcrest Cemetery highlights the emotional toll this loss had on Dr. Yarborough, who, despite his tireless efforts to keep Cary healthy, was unable to save his own daughter.

Dr. Yarborough's house includes both the family residence, which faces Academy Street, and an attached physician's office, which faces East Park Street. As Cary's physician during segregation, Dr. Yarborough was required to provide separate entrances for white and African American patients. However, he cleverly circumvented Jim Crow laws by having both entrances lead into a single waiting room. From East Park Street, the two staircases that once led to the separate entrances are still visible, although one door has been replaced by a window.

The home remains privately owned by Dr. Yarborough's family, and his renovated physician's office is now available for booking as a vacation rental.

Miss Esther Ivey's House

At 302 South Academy Street stands a home built around 1890, most famously known as the residence of Esther Ivey, a beloved Cary resident born the same year the house was constructed. The home is a symbol of a time when Cary first gained national recognition as the Gourd Capital of the World.

Although Esther Ivey was not a founding member of the Cary Gourd Society, she became a dedicated and active participant. Like many of the society's members, she endeavored to grow gourds in her own yard. However, the region's tough red clay soil proved difficult for gourd cultivation. Undeterred, Ivey adapted by creating raised garden beds in her backyard, which allowed her to successfully grow the gourds she loved and helped put the town she loved on the national map.

Cary's journey to becoming the Gourd Capital of the World is a story that intertwines community creativity, historical pride and a long-standing

Above: Esther Ivey's house. *Author's collection.*

Left: Esther Ivey holds gourd lamp made for festival. *Digital NC.*

Opposite: Cary town seal, adopted in 1964. *Page-Walker Historical Collection.*

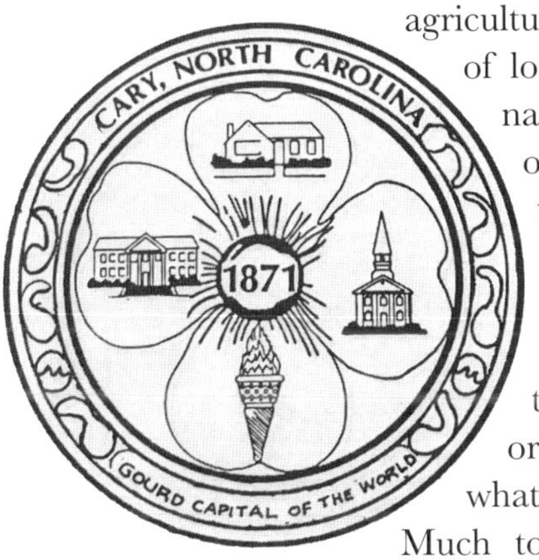

agricultural tradition. It began with a small group of local women in the 1930s and grew into a nationally recognized title that became part of Cary's very identity, even influencing the design of its town seal.

In 1934, a group of Cary women were intrigued by several magazine articles they had read about gourds. Inspired, they decided to buy a packet of mixed ornamental seeds and split them up to see what they could grow in their home gardens. Much to their surprise, the gourds flourished, growing in such abundance that they decided to take their hobby to the next level. Eager to continue their experiment, they contacted the International Gourd Society to obtain more exotic seeds. These women, later known as the "Gourd Gardeners," became pioneers in Cary's gourd legacy.

The initial success of their gardening experiment culminated in 1937 when the Gourd Gardeners made their public debut at the North Carolina State Fair. The group created an impressive display of their finest gourds, which generated considerable excitement. The success of their exhibit sparked the idea for an official club, and on December 27, 1937, the Gourd Gardeners became formalized. This marked the beginning of Cary's long association with gourd culture. The original members included Mrs. Mary Wilkinson, president; Mrs. Annie Maynard, vice-president; Mrs. Rachel Dunham, secretary-treasurer; Miss Mossa Eaton; Mrs. Annie Brower; Mrs. Ann McLean; and Mrs. Elizabeth Rood.

Soon after their establishment, the Gourd Gardeners' passion for crafting and exhibiting their gourds spread beyond local fairs. They quickly became known for their craftsmanship, making various items from gourds, including birdhouses, toys, jewelry, crockery, purses, baskets and even lamps. The innovative use of gourds in both practical and decorative items made their work stand out.

By 1938, Cary's gourd enthusiasts had gained such a reputation that they were invited to join the American Gourd Society. Cary became home to the society's Alpha Chapter, the first chapter in the nation. This recognition motivated the members to declare Cary the Gourd Capital of the World, a title that the town would proudly hold for many years.

stration Club
, September
e Methodist
esta Evans
meeting.
charge of
e on cloth-
aters.
onsor
ew on
l-out,
will

Gourd Village Garden Club

***Members of Gourd Village Garden Club** smile in anticipation of the big day coming*
First row, left to right: **Ricky Rood, Anna Young, Terrine Woodlief, Elva Templ**
Mary Johnson, Molly Poe, Mrs. Bernie Britt, Elizabeth Tyson. Second row: Marvin Joh
Julian Ray, Barbara Garrison, Connie Troutman, Sue Ross, Jess Heater, Ruth Ferg

Members of Cary's Gourd Village Garden Club. *Digital NC.*

The Gourd Gardeners did not stop there. They began sending their work to other states, notably winning prizes at a California festival, which further solidified Cary's reputation in the gourd world. The recognition Cary received from these external festivals helped the town garner nationwide attention for its unique contribution to agricultural and craft heritage.

As Cary's fame as the gourd capital grew, so did the need to celebrate it locally. Thus, the annual Cary Gourd Festival was born, the first of its kind in the South. Held for the first time in 1939, the festival became an opportunity for residents to showcase their creativity and craftsmanship with gourds. Attendees could see firsthand the wide range of items that could be made from gourds. After this successful showing, the group changed their name to the Gourd Village Garden Club of Cary.

The festival quickly became the longest-running annual event in Cary, drawing visitors from near and far. Each year brought a new theme, with participants pushing the boundaries of what could be done with gourds. Themes included everything from "Mother Goose gourds" to "gourds as holiday decorations," with participants creating everything from gourd snowmen to Christmas ornaments.

During World War II, gourd gardens were converted into Victory Gardens, and no gourd festivals were held. The few gourds that were grown were sent to hospitals, where convalescing soldiers used them for crafts. Additionally, Afghans featuring gourd designs were made for soldiers. In 1947, the Gourd Festival was revived, drawing thousands of visitors to admire handcrafted gourd displays. Among the creations were a Humpty-Dumpty gourd, Cinderella in a gourd coach drawn by mice with pear-shaped gourd bodies, a balloon-gourd lady doorstop holding a basket of mini-ornamentals and Native American–inspired recreations. The creativity and talent on display in Cary prompted cheeky exclamations of "Good Gourd!" and "Praise the Gourd!" according to articles penned at the time.

By the 1950s, the festivals held in today's Crosstown Pub had become so popular that they attracted national attention. A 1952 festival, for instance, featured a "Calendar with Gourds" theme, showcasing innovative gourd designs that corresponded with different months and holidays. This creativity helped elevate the festival beyond a local event into something that attracted tourists and gourd enthusiasts from across the United States.

Gourd Festival, 1947. *Page-Walker Historical Collection.*

Cary's deep connection to gourds wasn't just celebrated at the annual festival. It also became enshrined in the town's official imagery. In 1964, the Cary Chamber of Commerce sponsored a contest to design the town's official seal. Marion Daugherty, a Cary resident, submitted a design that featured ornamental gourds around the border. Her design reflected the pride the town took in its unique heritage, and it was selected as the winning entry, for which Mrs. Daugherty received a twenty-five-dollar war bond presented by then Chamber of Commerce President Ralph Ashworth. The inclusion of gourds on the town's seal symbolized their importance to Cary's identity at the time.

For many years, Cary's seal proudly bore this gourd-laden design, reminding everyone of the town's status as the Gourd Capital of the World. Although the town seal was eventually redesigned, and the gourds were replaced with curlicues, the influence of Cary's gourd heritage can still be seen in the design today. The original seal remains a part of the town's history, symbolizing a time when gourds were at the heart of the community.

While Cary no longer officially holds the title of Gourd Capital of the World, the legacy of its gourd history continues to thrive. The North Carolina Gourd Society, which was founded in Cary as the Alpha Chapter, remains active today. The society holds an annual festival at the North Carolina State Fairgrounds in Raleigh, where gourd enthusiasts gather to celebrate the rich cultural and crafting traditions associated with gourds. Although the festival has moved from Cary to Raleigh, its roots remain deeply connected to Cary's history.

And Esther Ivey's home on Academy Street, now a privately owned business, is another enduring symbol of that legacy in downtown Cary.

Ivey-Ellington House

The Ivey-Ellington House is a significant historical landmark in Cary, dating to the 1870s. Originally located on West Chatham Street, the house is one of Cary's oldest surviving structures, making it an essential part of the town's heritage. Despite its Gothic cottage style, it has never served as a church, but instead always a family residence. Early deeds suggest that the Ivey-Ellington House was built circa 1875, when Frank Page sold the land to A.T. Mise. The property changed ownership several times before being sold to Thaddeus and Mary Ivey around 1893. During this time, Thaddeus worked

Above: Ivey-Ellington House in original Chatham Street location. *Page-Walker Arts and History Center/Leslie Douglas.*

Left: The Ivey-Ellington House in its original location as seen from The Walk Up. *Author's collection.*

as an assistant to the state treasurer in Raleigh, commuting by train from Cary to Raleigh.

At its original location on West Chatham Street, the home was known to farmers as a friendly resting stop as they took their cattle to market in Raleigh. They would stop over in the front yard of the house and take water in the Iveys' well. Sometimes turkeys came with the cattle, and they would roost in the trees around downtown Cary.

In 1898, Thaddeus and Mary Ivey sold the house to C.R. Scott, who owned it until 1918. That year, Scott sold the property to Joseph A. Smith, who held it for less than a year before selling it to J. Harrison Ellington. The Ellington family lived in the house from 1918 until 1946. After J. Harrison Ellington's death, his widow and heirs were forced to sell the property.

As Cary grew, the building found itself increasingly encroached by modern developments on Chatham Street. In 2023, the Town of Cary moved the Ivey-Ellington House to a more prominent location on South Academy Street across from the Downtown Cary Park to avoid its demolition from development. The house completed restoration and rehabilitation to become Downtown Cary Park offices in May 2025 and likely will be open to the public for limited access. Because the land was part of the home's original historic status, the relocation caused the home to lose its designation in the National Register of Historic Places.

The historic homes along Academy Street collectively tell the story of Cary's evolution. Thankfully, many of these homes still stand today, offering a glimpse into the past, and their stories deserve to be shared. The ongoing preservation efforts by both private owners and the town not only protect these homes' legacies but also cultivate a sense of pride among Cary's residents, serving as a bridge between the town's past and present. When next walking Academy Street, perhaps it will now be easier to appreciate the layers of history embedded in these homes and the stories they hold.

Conclusion

One of the most remarkable aspects of Cary's hidden history is its population growth—a story of transformation that mirrors its evolution from a small village to one of the fastest-growing towns in the United States. Numbers alone tell a compelling tale:

Year	Cary's Approximate Population
1880	316
1890	423
1900	333
1910	383
1920	645
1930	909
1940	1,141
1950	1,446
1960	3,356
1970	7,339
1980	21,708
1990	43,461
2000	97,411
2010	135,234
2020	174,721
2025 (estimate)	191,000

These figures highlight the extraordinary changes Cary has experienced, especially in the past century. From a modest town of fewer than 1,000 residents in 1930, Cary has grown to a bustling community approaching 200,000 today. This trajectory is both a testament to the area's appeal and a reflection of its resilience in adapting to economic, cultural and demographic shifts. With just 316 residents in 1880, Cary maintained a small-town feel through the early twentieth century, with modest growth to 1,141 by 1940. However, starting in the 1960s, Cary began experiencing unprecedented expansion, with the population tripling between 1960 and 1970, driven by the establishment of the Research Triangle Park (RTP). By 2020, Cary's population had reached 174,721, a striking increase of more than 55,000 people in just two decades.

Cary's development has been influenced by several factors, including its proximity to RTP, a strong emphasis on quality education and intentional urban planning. The town is recognized for its high educational attainment levels, with nearly 70 percent of residents holding a college degrees and over 25 percent an advanced degree. According to the town's 2025 State of Cary report, Cary's population comprises more than sixty nationalities, with 24.7 percent born outside of the United States: 56 percent white, 19 percent Asian, 11.5 percent Hispanic and 7.8 percent African American. Cary remains a magnet for professionals and families seeking quality schools and safe neighborhoods. This influx has led to further development and quality of life amenities, reinforcing its appeal.

The challenges that accompany such rapid growth are many. Cary's journey has not been perfect, nor has its progress been without contention. There is an inherent tension between preserving the small-town charm and identity that originally drew people to the area and managing the demands of an expanding population. As Cary has developed into a hub of innovation and opportunity, its leadership and residents have faced the ongoing task of maintaining the character and traditions that make the town unique and successful.

Today, Cary represents a fascinating case study of sustainable suburban growth. Its population, estimated at nearly 191,000 in 2025, underscores its continued evolution. The story of Cary's growth illustrates the need for a delicate balance of progress and preservation, with the hope that its rich history remains apparent in its present and future.

This balancing act can be described as the "goose and the golden egg dilemma." Cary's success—its thriving economy, desirable quality of life and cultural vitality—has attracted newcomers from all over the world. Yet

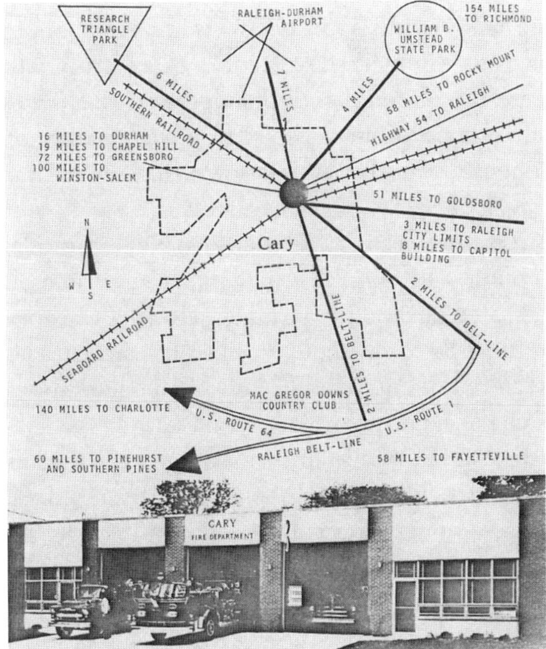

Marketing Cary as a place to live to IBM employees. *Digital NC.*

the town must be cautious not to let the very factors that made it attractive be overshadowed or diminished by the pressures of growth. Infrastructure, green spaces, historic preservation and community vitality remain pivotal in ensuring that Cary continues to thrive while honoring its roots.

THROUGHOUT THIS BOOK, I have shared and explored the lesser-known stories and history that have shaped Cary. From its earliest days as a small village with deep agricultural roots to its pivotal moments during the Civil War, in public education and innovative community development, Cary's history is rich with narratives of perseverance, resilience, vision and community spirit. Its history is full of such examples, as well as physical structures that can still be seen today. The town's remaining historical landmarks, in downtown and beyond, serve as enduring reminders of this history and people. Efforts by local historians, preservationists and community organizations ensure that Cary's past is not forgotten, even as the skyline and demographics continue to evolve.

In tracing Cary's growth, it is clear that it is not just a story of numbers, but a reflection of broader trends in American history. The town's transition from the place in between Raleigh and points west to the second-largest town in America mirrors the post–World War II suburbanization boom seen consistently across the country. Similarly, its recent decades of growth echo the rise of technology-driven economies and the migration of families and professionals seeking better opportunities and prioritizing quality of life living. Now Cary is no longer a suburb, but is a town that serves as a destination in and of itself.

As Cary continues to grow, so too does its potential to serve as a model for other communities grappling with similar challenges. How does a town embrace progress while safeguarding its heritage? How can history inform decisions about the future? By knowing Cary's history, hidden and otherwise, we as Caryites are all better equipped to answer these questions as we along with our leaders chart the path forward.

This book aims to celebrate Cary's unique history, recognizing that its identity is deeply tied to the stories of its people, places and milestones. By shining a light on these lesser-known aspects of Cary's past, I hope to deepen appreciation for what makes the town special and inspire a sense of stewardship among current and future residents.

The stories captured in these pages are more than just historical accounts—they are touchstones for understanding Cary's unique personality and narrative and its important contributions to the rest of North Carolina and even the nation. By remembering our roots, we can better navigate where we are headed. Cary's success is not just in its ability to grow, but in its history to ensure that growth is guided thoughtfully, by the values and traditions that have defined it since its founding.

Let this book also serve as a reminder that history is not static. It is a living, breathing narrative that evolves with discovery and time. I have uncovered and reported on newly discovered history and updated some past accounts. But history has a way of always revealing itself—especially Cary's history, it seems! As this surely continues, I am excited by these new discoveries that can only enrich our understanding of Cary and its history. Cary's past, present and future should be dynamic and interconnected, each informing and enriching the other. By honoring the town's history and sharing its stories, I hope to ensure that Cary's legacy remains vibrant and present—not only in memory but also in practice.

Cary's history may have been hidden in plain sight, but now, illuminated and celebrated, it has the power to inspire and guide as the town continues to grow and flourish. May the past always have a place in the present, ensuring that Cary's story is one of innovation, ambition, resilience, vibrancy and pride for generations to come.

Bibliography

Amis, Moses N. "Historical Raleigh with Sketches of Wake County." Carolana, 1913. https://www.carolana.com.

Beil, H. Charles. "Theodosia: Cache #3 of the Buried Treasure Caches of Treasure Man (H Charles Beil)." Mysterious Writings. https://mysteriouswritings.com.

Brewer, Ashley. "Camp Polk Prison Farm, Park Creation, and Racial Segregation: Seeing the History of William B. Umstead State Park's Land through Maps, Plats, and Plans." Digital NC, April 17, 2024. https://www.digitalnc.org.

Byrd, Thomas M. "Research Notes Folder 3—Anecdotes and Incidents." Digital NC. https://lib.digitalnc.org.

———. "Research Notes Folder 4—Early Developments." Digital NC. https://lib.digitalnc.org.

———. "Research Notes Folder 5—Beautification." Digital NC. https://lib.digitalnc.org.

———. "Research Notes Folder 6—Civil War." Digital NC. https://lib.digitalnc.org.

———. "Research Notes Folder 7—Distinguished Citizens." Digital NC. https://lib.digitalnc.org.

———. "Research Notes Folder 8—Chapter V, Economic Activity and Houses." Digital NC. https://lib.digitalnc.org.

———. "Research Notes Folder 9—Economic Activity Since Centennial." Digital NC. https://lib.digitalnc.org.

———. "Research Notes Folder 10—Education Since 1950." Digital NC. https://lib.digitalnc.org.

———. "Research Notes Folder 11—Deeds, Land Grants, and Other Land Records." Digital NC. https://lib.digitalnc.org.

———. "Research Notes Folder 12—Events." Digital NC. https://lib.digitalnc.org.

———. "Research Notes Folder 14—General Information." Digital NC. https://lib.digitalnc.org.

———. "Research Notes Folder 15—Jones Family." Digital NC. https://lib.digitalnc.org.

———. "Research Notes Folder 16—Manners and Morals." Digital NC. https://lib.digitalnc.org.

———. "Research Notes Folder 17—Municipal Developments Since the Centennial." Digital NC. https://lib.digitalnc.org.

———. "Research Notes Folder 20—Parks, Recreation, Events." Digital NC. https://lib.digitalnc.org.

———. "Research Notes Folder 21—Chapter IX, Municipal Growth Prior to Centennial." Digital NC. https://lib.digitalnc.org.

———. "Research Notes Folder 22—Page Family." Digital NC. https://lib.digitalnc.org.

———. "Research Notes Folder 23—Walter Hines Page." Digital NC. https://lib.digitalnc.org.

———. "Research Notes Folder 24—Page Deeds." Digital NC. https://lib.digitalnc.org.

———. "Research Notes Folder 25—Elizabeth Reid Murray Correspondence." Digital NC. https://lib.digitalnc.org.

———. "Research Notes Folder 26—Samuel Cary." Digital NC. https://lib.digitalnc.org.

———. "Research Notes Folder 28—Preserving the Past." Digital NC. https://lib.digitalnc.org.

———. "Research Notes Folder 29—Templeton Family." Digital NC. https://lib.digitalnc.org.

———. "Research Notes Folder 30—Sources, Corresponding, Pictures, Biography." Digital NC. https://lib.digitalnc.org.

———. "Research Notes Folder 31—Who We Are Census." Digital NC. https://lib.digitalnc.org.

———. "Research Notes Folder 32—Centennial Pictures, Brochures, Drawings." Digital NC. https://lib.digitalnc.org.

———. "Research Notes Folder 33—Cary Planning Photos." Digital NC. https://lib.digitalnc.org.

Byrd, Thomas M., and Evelyn Holland. *Cary's 100th Anniversary*. Cary Area Centennial Corporation, 1971.

Byrd, Thomas M., and Jerry Miller. *Around and About Cary*. Daniel Industries Inc., 1970.

———. *Around and About Cary*. Edwards Brothers Inc., 1994.

Chamberlain, Hope Summerell. "History of Wake County, North Carolina, with Sketches of Those Who Have Most Influenced Its Development." Library of Congress, 1922. https://www.loc.gov/item/23000876.

Charlotte News. "Site for Fair Is Finally Approved." November 16, 1927, 9.

Clapper, Patti. "Frank Page's Will Attached." Raleigh, North Carolina, December 21, 2023.

Crow, Jeffrey J. "North Carolina Cary Historic District." National Archive Catalogue, March 23, 2001. https://catalog.archives.gov.

Daniels, Dennis F. "Historical Research Report: Polk Prison Property." North Carolina Digital Collections, August 31, 2001. https://digital.ncdcr.gov.

Durham Sun. "Mr. Page's Funeral." October 18, 1899, 4.

———. "Page-McLeod Nuptials." November 17, 1898, 4.

Engram, Barbara. "The Arrington Jones Story." Cary, North Carolina, September 30, 2020.

———. "The Evans/Bailey Story." Cary, North Carolina, September 30.

Find a Grave. "Allison Francis 'Frank' Page." https://www.findagrave.com.

Friends of the Page-Walker. "Cary Me Back." https://friendsofpagewalker.wildapricot.org.

———. Oral History Project—Audio Files, July 25, 2012. https://friendsofpagewalker.wildapricot.org.

———. Oral History Project—Transcripts, March 19, 2009. https://drive.google.com/file/d/1SK-XYWrlqs_BGwwRDVVKpratx8bI8XAA/view.

———. Oral History Project—Transcripts, March 31, 2009. https://drive.google.com/file/d/15CdG8xU1jseN-mmWm_9Pr4fsCymRlbal/view.

———. "Walking Tour Hillcrest Cemetery." May 2016. https://cdn.wildapricot.com.

Hamilton, Mary Hicks. "Here's Wake Ghost Story." *News & Observer*, July 8, 1951, 50.

Henrick, Burton J. *The Life and Letters of Walter Hines Page*: Doubleday, Page & Company, 1925.

Hill, Michael. "National Register of Historic Places: Nancy Jones House." State of North Carolina, October 20, 1983. https://files.nc.gov/ncdcr/nr/WA0187.pdf.

Historical Marker Database. "Dr. Frank R. Yarborough House." September 19, 2023. https://www.hmdb.org.

———. "Sams-Jones House." September 21, 2023. https://www.hmdb.org.

Leah, Heather. "In Plain Sight: Miniature 'Redwood Forest' Hidden in Downtown Cary." WRAL, April 29, 2023. https://www.wral.com.

Loflin, Katherine, and Carla Michaels. "Clippings About the PW Hotel for Dating." March 10, 2024.

McKnight, David. "Landmark's Caretaker, 'No More Fire, No More House.'" *Herald-Sun*, September 23, 1970, 3.

Michaels, Carla Jordan. "Dating the Page Walker." Cary, North Carolina, March 13, 2024.

Morning Post. "Funeral of Mr. A.F. Page." October 18, 1899, 7.

———. "Page-Wynne Nuptials." February 2, 1902, 3.

———. "Will of Late A.F. Page." October 22, 1899, 5.

Murray, Elizabeth Reid. "Wake, Capital County of North Carolina, Volume 1: Prehistory through Centennial." Digital NC, 1983. https://lib.digitalnc.org.

Mysterious Writings. "In Search of the Theodosia Cache of H Charles Beil (Treasure Man): Six Questions with Jason Griffin." https://mysteriouswritings.com.

Nashville Graphic. "Cary, N.C., Whence the Name." May 25, 1911, 3.

News & Observer. "As Raleigh Grew from the Forest." June 6, 1907, 50.

———. "Booze Coming to Cary." April 25, 1964, 18.

———. "Cary's Public High School Was First in North Carolina." May 18, 1940, 32.

———. "Engineer Fetner Dies at Hamlet." November 29, 1925, 2.

———. "Fire Destroyed House of Former Ambassador." April 18, 1971, 92.

———. "Honor to His Ashes." December 29, 1893, 1.

———. "Maynard Makes Visit to Cary High School." November 7, 1919, 14.

———. "Mr. Frank Page No Better." October 13, 1899, 8.

———. "Stone Laid for Masonic Temple." July 22, 1931, 4.

———. "This UNC Head Wasn't Popular." September 3, 1950, 48.
———. "Town of Cary Boasts N.C.'s First Paved Road." April 18, 1971, 89.
North Carolinian. "Consul General Jones." January 4, 1894, 2.
Oakwood Cemetery. "Search Burial Records." https://historicoakwoodcemetery.org.
Page, Allison Francis. "Who Wants to Make Money." *Spirit of the Age*, July 13, 1859, 3.
Patrick, Jessica. "History: Cary, the Gourd Capital of the World." *Cary Citizen*, August 4, 2015. https://carycitizenarchive.com.
Press-Visitor. "Death of Mrs. A.F. Page." August 23, 1897, 1.
Prison News 4, no. 1. "Camp Polk Items" (1930): 3.
R.M. "On President Lincoln's Death." *Daily Standard*, April 19, 1865, 2.
Scoyoc, Peggy Van. "Cary's Heritage: Barnabus Jones Farm, Pt. 1." *Cary Citizen*, March 14, 2019. https://carycitizenarchive.com.
———. "Desegregating Cary." *Passing Time Press*, 2010.
———. "Just a Horse-Stopping Place." 2006. Lulu.com.
Spanbauer, Rebecca. "Application for Historic Landmark Designation: Guess-Ogle House." Town of Cary, June 2, 2008. https://www.carync.gov.
St. Louis Globe-Democrat. "Died on a 'Hoodooed' Ship." December 18, 1893, 1.
State of North Carolina. "Private Laws of the State of North-Carolina, Passed by the General Assembly [1870–71]." North Carolina Digital Collections, April 3, 1871. https://digital.ncdcr.gov.
Terrell, Virginia L. "Cary Honors Man Who Kept It from Being 'Bull City.'" *News & Observer*, October 28, 1923, 35.
Town of Cary. "Cary Newsletter: Cary History Minute." July 2018. https://aquastar.townofcary.org.
———. "Local Historic Landmarks." https://www.carync.gov.
———. "National Register Properties in Cary." https://www.carync.gov.
Town of Cary Planning Department. "Thomason and Associates." Historic Preservation Master Plan, May 27, 2010. https://thomasonandassociates.com.
"Treasure De-Layered Map." Apex, North Carolina, February 7, 2024. In author's possession.
Wagner, Heather M. "National Register of Historic Places—Ivey-Ellington House." National Archive Catalogue, March 27, 2008. https://catalog.archives.gov.

Williams-Vinson, Ella Arrington. "Both Sides of the Tracks: A Profile of the Colored Community, Cary, North Carolina." 1996.

———. "Both Sides of the Tracks II: Recollections of Cary, North Carolina, 1860–2000." 2001.

Worth, Nicholas. *The Southerner*. Doubleday, Page & Company, 1909.

About the Author

Dr. Katherine Loflin, "The City Doctor," is an award-winning trailblazer on how people connect with places and the relationship to local economic development and individual well-being. As a trusted advisor to global leaders and communities for nearly two decades, her work has been credited for helping to improve the quality of life for millions around the world. Dr. Loflin is a multiple TEDx speaker and internationally recognized keynote presenter. As founder of The City Doctor Productions, she creates acclaimed tours, events and productions that bring local history to life. Her entertainment credits include roles as an ABC executive producer, playwright, director and actress. Dr. Loflin also currently serves as Cary's history ambassador and vice-chair of its Historic Preservation Commission and is a member of the Daughters of the American Revolution. Dr. Loflin is a North Carolina native and a direct descendant of one of the state's recognized founding families, who settled in North Carolina before 1729. She holds a PhD in social work from UNC–Chapel Hill and lives in Cary, North Carolina.